The Task of Economics

FORTY-FIFTH ANNUAL REPORT
A RECORD FOR 1964 AND PLANS FOR 1965

NATIONAL BUREAU OF ECONOMIC RESEARCH, INC.
261 MADISON AVENUE / NEW YORK, N. Y. 10016

COPYRIGHT© 1965 BY
NATIONAL BUREAU OF ECONOMIC RESEARCH, INC.
261 MADISON AVENUE, NEW YORK, N. Y. 10016

ALL RIGHTS RESERVED

The National Bureau of Economic Research was organized in 1920 in response to a growing demand for objective determination of the facts bearing upon economic problems, and for their interpretation in an impartial manner. The National Bureau concentrates on topics of national importance that are susceptible to scientific treatment.

The National Bureau seeks not merely to determine and interpret important economic facts, but to do so under such auspices and with such safeguards as shall make its findings carry conviction to all sections of the nation.

No report of the Research Staff may be published without the approval of the Board of Directors. Rigid provisions guard the National Bureau from becoming a source of profit to its members, directors, or officers, and from becoming an agency for propaganda.

By issuing its findings in the form of scientific reports, entirely divorced from recommendations on policy, the National Bureau hopes to aid all thoughtful men, however divergent their views on public policy, to base their discussions upon objective knowledge as distinguished from subjective opinion.

The National Bureau assumes no obligation toward present or future contributors except to determine, interpret, and publish economic facts for the benefit of the nation at large, and to provide contributors with copies of its publications.

RELATION OF THE DIRECTORS TO THE WORK AND PUBLICATIONS OF THE NATIONAL BUREAU OF ECONOMIC RESEARCH

1. The object of the National Bureau of Economic Research is to ascertain and to present to the public important economic facts and their interpretation in a scientific and impartial manner. The Board of Directors is charged with the responsibility of ensuring that the work of the National Bureau is carried on in strict conformity with this object.

2. To this end the Board of Directors shall appoint one or more Directors of Research.

3. The Director or Directors of Research shall submit to the members of the Board, or to its Executive Committee, for their formal adoption, all specific proposals concerning researches to be instituted.

4. No report shall be published until the Director or Directors of Research shall have submitted to the Board a summary drawing attention to the character of the data and their utilization in the report, the nature and treatment of the problems involved, the main conclusions, and such other information as in their opinion would serve to determine the suitability of the report for publication in accordance with the principles of the National Bureau.

5. A copy of any manuscript proposed for publication shall also be submitted to each member of the Board. For each manuscript to be so submitted a special committee shall be appointed by the President, or at his designation by the Executive Director, consisting of three Directors selected as nearly as may be one from each general division of the Board. The names of the special manuscript committee shall be stated to each Director when the summary and report described in paragraph (4) are sent to him. It shall be the duty of each member of the committee to read the manuscript. If each member of the special committee signifies his approval within thirty days, the manuscript may be published. If each member of the special committee has not signified his approval within thirty days of the transmittal of the report and manuscript, the Director of Research shall then notify each member of the Board, requesting approval or disapproval of publication, and thirty additional days shall be granted for this purpose. The manuscript shall then not be published unless at least a majority of the entire Board and a two-thirds majority of those members of the Board who shall have voted on the proposal within the time fixed for the receipt of votes on the publication proposed shall have approved.

6. No manuscript may be published, though approved by each member of the special committee, until forty-five days have elapsed from the transmittal of the summary and report. The interval is allowed for the receipt of any memorandum of dissent or reservation, together with a brief statement of his reasons, that any member may wish to express; and such memorandum of dissent or reservation shall be published with the manuscript if he so desires. Publication does not, however, imply that each member of the Board has read the manuscript, or that either members of the Board in general, or of the special committee, have passed upon its validity in every detail.

7. A copy of this resolution shall, unless otherwise determined by the Board, be printed in each copy of every National Bureau book.

(Resolution adopted October 25, 1926,
as revised February 6, 1933, and February 24, 1941)

NATIONAL BUREAU OF ECONOMIC RESEARCH

OFFICERS
Frank W. Fetter, *Chairman*
Arthur F. Burns, *President*
Theodore O. Yntema, *Vice-President*
Donald B. Woodward, *Treasurer*
Solomon Fabricant, *Director of Research*
Geoffrey H. Moore, *Associate Director of Research*
Hal B. Lary, *Associate Director of Research*
William J. Carson, *Executive Director*

DIRECTORS AT LARGE
Robert B. Anderson, *New York City*
Wallace J. Campbell, *Nationwide Insurance*
Erwin D. Canham, *Christian Science Monitor*
Solomon Fabricant, *New York University*
Marion B. Folsom, *Eastman Kodak Company*
Crawford H. Greenewalt, *E. I. du Pont de Nemours & Company*
Gabriel Hauge, *Manufacturers Hanover Trust Company*
A. J. Hayes, *International Association of Machinists*
Walter W. Heller, *University of Minnesota*
Albert J. Hettinger, Jr., *Lazard Frères and Company*
Nicholas Kelley, *Kelley Drye Newhall Maginnes & Warren*
H. W. Laidler, *League for Industrial Democracy*
Geoffrey H. Moore, *National Bureau of Economic Research*
Charles G. Mortimer, *General Foods Corporation*
J. Wilson Newman, *Dun & Bradstreet, Inc.*
George B. Roberts, *Larchmont, New York*
Harry Scherman, *Book-of-the-Month Club*
Boris Shishkin, *American Federation of Labor and Congress of Industrial Organizations*
George Soule, *South Kent, Connecticut*
Gus Tyler, *International Ladies' Garment Workers' Union*
Joseph H. Willits, *Langhorne, Pennsylvania*
Donald B. Woodward, *A. W. Jones and Company*

DIRECTORS BY UNIVERSITY APPOINTMENT
V. W. Bladen, *Toronto*
Francis M. Boddy, *Minnesota*
Arthur F. Burns, *Columbia*
Lester V. Chandler, *Princeton*
Melvin G. de Chazeau, *Cornell*
Frank W. Fetter, *Northwestern*
R. A. Gordon, *California*
Harold M. Groves, *Wisconsin*
Gottfried Haberler, *Harvard*
Maurice W. Lee, *North Carolina*
Lloyd G. Reynolds, *Yale*
Paul A. Samuelson, *Massachusetts Institute of Technology*
Theodore W. Schultz, *Chicago*
Willis J. Winn, *Pennsylvania*

DIRECTORS BY APPOINTMENT OF OTHER ORGANIZATIONS
Percival F. Brundage, *American Institute of Certified Public Accountants*
Nathaniel Goldfinger, *American Federation of Labor and Congress of Industrial Organizations*
Harold G. Halcrow, *American Farm Economic Association*
Murray Shields, *American Management Association*
Willard L. Thorp, *American Economic Association*
W. Allen Wallis, *American Statistical Association*
Harold F. Williamson, *Economic History Association*
Theodore O. Yntema, *Committee for Economic Development*

DIRECTORS EMERITI
Shepard Morgan, *Norfolk, Connecticut*   N. I. Stone, *New York City*
Jacob Viner, *Princeton, New Jersey*

RESEARCH STAFF
Moses Abramovitz
Gary S. Becker
William H. Brown, Jr.
Gerhard Bry
Arthur F. Burns
Phillip Cagan
Frank G. Dickinson
James S. Earley
Richard A. Easterlin
Solomon Fabricant
Albert Fishlow
Milton Friedman
Victor R. Fuchs
H. G. Georgiadis
Raymond W. Goldsmith
Jack M. Guttentag
Challis A. Hall, Jr.
Daniel M. Holland
Thor Hultgren
F. Thomas Juster
C. Harry Kahn
John W. Kendrick
Irving B. Kravis
Hal B. Lary
Robert E. Lipsey
Ruth P. Mack
Jacob Mincer
Ilse Mintz
Geoffrey H. Moore
Roger F. Murray
Ralph L. Nelson
G. Warren Nutter
Richard T. Selden
Lawrence H. Seltzer
Robert P. Shay
George J. Stigler
Norman B. Ture
Herbert B. Woolley
Victor Zarnowitz

Contents

		PAGE
PART I.	THE TASK OF ECONOMICS — SOLOMON FABRICANT	1
PART II.	REPORTS ON SELECTED BUREAU PROGRAMS	5
	Some Implications of the Growing Importance of the Service Industries — Victor R. Fuchs	5
	On the Accuracy and Properties of Short-Term Economic Forecasts — Victor Zarnowitz	16
	Consumer Credit Markets: A Progress Report — Robert P. Shay	25
PART III.	STUDIES NEW AND COMPLETED	33
	New Studies	33
	Studies Completed	35
PART IV.	STAFF REPORTS ON RESEARCH UNDER WAY	39
	1. Economic Growth	39
	Tax Policies for Economic Growth	39
	Survey of the Use of Alternative Depreciation Methods Under the Internal Revenue Code of 1954 — Norman B. Ture	40
	Corporate Profits Taxation and Economic Growth — Challis A. Hall	44

	PAGE
Effect of Changes in Tax Laws on Modernization Expenditures in the Textile Industry — Thomas M. Stanback, Jr.	45
Personal Capital Gains Taxation and Economic Growth — Roger F. Miller	46
The Tax Treatment of Fluctuating Incomes — C. Harry Kahn	47
Effect of Taxation on Personal Effort — Daniel M. Holland	47
Productivity in the Service Industries — Victor R. Fuchs	48
Productivity Growth in Distribution — David Schwartzman	49
State and Local Governments — Ernest Kurnow	50
Barber and Beauty Shops — Jean Wilburn	51
Long Swings in the Growth of Population and Labor Force — Richard A. Easterlin	52
Long Swings in Urban Building Activity — Manuel Gottlieb	53
Economic Growth of the Soviet Union — G. Warren Nutter	54
Use of Labor in Soviet Agriculture — Douglas B. Diamond	54
Other Studies	55
2. National Income, Consumption, and Capital Formation	55
Investment in Education — Gary S. Becker	55
Consumer Purchase Plans — F. Thomas Juster	56
The Impact of Public and Private Pension Systems on Saving and Investment — Roger F. Murray	57
Projections of Private Pension Plans, 1962-82 — Daniel M. Holland	57
Philanthropy in the American Economy — Frank G. Dickinson	57
Estimates of Private Giving — Ralph L. Nelson	58
Other Studies	58
3. Business Cycles	59
General Studies	59
Study of Short-Term Economic Forecasting — Victor Zarnowitz	59
Econometric Model Forecasts — Jon Cunnyngham	60
Recognition of Cyclical Turning Points — Rendigs Fels	64
Business Cycle Indicators — Julius Shiskin and Geoffrey H. Moore	64
GNP Revisions and Forecasting Accuracy — Rosanne Cole	66
Statistical Indicators — Geoffrey H. Moore	67

	PAGE
Fluctuation in Stocks of Purchased Materials on Hand and on Order — Ruth P. Mack	68
Labor Turnover — Charlotte Boschan	70
Money and Banking — Milton Friedman and Anna J. Schwartz	72
Source Book of Statistics Relating to Investment — Robert E. Lipsey and Doris Preston	72
Electronic Computer Applications — Gerhard Bry and Charlotte Boschan	72
Other Studies	73

4. Financial Institutions and Processes ... 73

Interest Rates	73
The Mortgage Market — Jack M. Guttentag	74
Yields on Direct Placements — Avery B. Cohan	75
Cyclical Behavior of Interest Rates — Phillip Cagan	76
Trends and Cycles in Corporate Bond and Stock Financing — George R. Morrison	76
Banking Markets and Bank Structure — Donald P. Jacobs and George R. Morrison	77
Consumer Credit — Robert P. Shay	77
Consumer Finances — F. Thomas Juster	78
Rate Structure in Automobile Financing — Robert P. Shay	79
Finance Rate Ceilings — Wallace P. Mors	79
The Quality of Credit in Booms and Depressions — James S. Earley	79
The Quality of Mortgage Credit — James S. Earley and John P. Herzog	81
Income from Employment Under the Personal Income Tax — C. Harry Kahn	82
Other Studies	82

5. International Economic Relations ... 82

Exports of Manufactures by Less Developed Countries — Hal B. Lary	82
United States Performance in International Trade — H. G. Georgiadis	87
International Price Comparison Study — Irving B. Kravis,	

	PAGE
Robert E. Lipsey, and Philip J. Bourque	87
Foreign Trade and Business Cycles — Ilse Mintz	88
Other Studies	90

PART V: CONFERENCES ON RESEARCH — 91

Conference on Research in Income and Wealth — 92
Universities-National Bureau Committee for Economic Research — 93
Conference on Measurement and Interpretation of Job Vacancies — 94
Visitors to the National Bureau — 95

PART VI: DIRECTORS, OFFICERS, AND RESEARCH STAFF — 97

PART VII: FINANCES AND SOURCES OF SUPPORT — 99

AUTHORS OF STUDIES COMPLETED OR IN PROCESS DURING 1964-65 — 101

NATIONAL BUREAU PUBLICATIONS — 105

CONTRIBUTIONS AND SUBSCRIPTIONS — 116

HOW NATIONAL BUREAU PUBLICATIONS ARE DISTRIBUTED:
HOW TO ORDER PUBLICATIONS — 117

PART I

The Task of Economics

Only recently, as the generations go, has the possibility of human progress been a serious question for hardheaded men.

To Malthus, at the close of the eighteenth century, the speculations of Condorcet and Godwin on the "perfectibility" of man and of society appeared "little better than a dream, a beautiful phantom of the imagination." "I ardently wish for such happy improvements," Malthus confessed, "but I see great, and, to my understanding, unconquerable difficulties in the way of them."

Vast changes already under way at the time Malthus wrote were greatly to alter the thinking of the practical men who came after him. By 1890, Alfred Marshall could say: "Now at last, we are setting ourselves seriously to inquire whether it is necessary that there should be any so-called 'lower classes' . . . whether it is really impossible that all should start in the world with a fair chance of leading a cultured life, free from the pains of poverty and the stagnating influences of excessive mechanical toil. . . . The question is being pressed to the front by the growing earnestness of the age."

What had "done more than anything else to give practical interest" to the question, Marshall noted, was "the steady progress of the working classes during the nineteenth century."

This progress has continued and perhaps even accelerated since Marshall wrote. Also, our age has grown still more "earnest." We no longer speak of the "lower classes." And we are much more confident. Even those still unsure of society's power to cope with its economic problems affirm the need to test its capacity with one or another social experiment or innovation. Today, most people would put Marshall's question less diffidently. Yet the words with which he opened his *Principles of Economics* may still serve to state, with sensible caution, the major economic question that engages our own generation, and not only in the "developed countries" but throughout the world.

Marshall went on to say that "the question cannot be fully answered by economic science.

... But the answer depends in a great measure upon facts and inferences, which are within the province of economics; and this it is which gives to economic studies their chief and their highest interest."

These words of Marshall may also serve us. They define the task and the responsibility that economists assume when they undertake research. It is their task to gather the economic facts and draw the inferences that can help answer the question Marshall posed, and help answer it in the only convincing way: by enlarging further the proportion of men and women who "start in the world with a fair chance." It is the responsibility of economists to provide facts and inferences that are both sound and relevant—facts and inferences on national income, consumption, and capital formation, on economic growth and business cycles, on financial affairs and international economic relations—facts and inferences that can command the credence of men of diverse views on how to improve the "fair chance" every human being deserves.

For us at the National Bureau, this has meant working during the past year, as in earlier years, as hard and as carefully as we could, on the several parts of the task that economists set themselves:

clarifying the concepts used in dealing with economic problems—for example, the concept of "credit quality," with which Earley is struggling, because we feel it to be important to an appraisal of the country's economic stability;

devising and testing economic measurements—for example, of the number of job vacancies, which, when compared with the number of unemployed, might help to throw light on the state of the aggregate demand for labor, as Burns mentioned in opening our recent conference on the measurement and interpretation of job vacancies;

compiling, in systematic form, significant facts on economic organization and change—for example, facts on the forms, terms, costs, and magnitudes of consumer finance, which has assumed a large role in today's economy, and on which Shay presents a progress report below;

describing and explaining economic behavior—for example, with respect to personal savings under the impact of growing public and private pension systems, the subject of a paper by Cagan now in the hands of the Board for review;

drawing the implications of changes in economic structure and organization—for example, the relative growth of the service industries, the subject of Fuchs' report;

providing useful clues to the future—as in the studies, critical and constructive, of forecasts of short-term economic change, on which Zarnowitz reports;

analyzing and comparing present and proposed policies—as in the study of wage and price guideposts we are planning as part of the new project on productivity, employment, and price levels.

What has been done during the year at the National Bureau is described more systematically in the other reports that follow: reports on studies completed and begun, in Part III; on the progress made in research under way, in Part IV; on research conferences planned and held, and on the publication schedules of the conference proceedings, in Part V. And as I have mentioned, three of my colleagues report more fully on the areas of research for which they carry chief responsibility. Their reports appear in Part II.

Before we turn to these, let me interject a note of caution concerning the expectations to which economic research may reasonably give rise. I shall use the words of our proposal for the project on productivity, employment, and price levels, which we are designing to study an important problem—the problem whether, or to what degree, trends in the price level are related to the advance of a nation's prosperity. In the more specific terms in which it is often put, the problem is whether, and if so how, a free society can achieve significant increases in productivity, reach and maintain reasonably full employment, and yet avoid inflation. In requesting support for the project, we stressed that "the problem of maintaining prosperity without inflation in a society that is basically free is surrounded by so many difficulties, political as well as economic, that too much must not be expected from any program of research.

No matter how well or skillfully it is done, it may still not provide definitive or generally acceptable answers. Before that state is reached, much further experimentation with monetary, fiscal, and other policy weapons may need to be carried out both by our government and other nations. It is a matter of considerable importance, however, what experiments will be undertaken and how they may be carried out. If nothing more, basic studies on relevant questions should help to provide some useful guidelines for future experiments and thus—it may be hoped—help to avoid serious mistakes of economic policy."

To help provide useful guidelines for economic policy, and thus to help avoid serious mistakes, is to help conquer some of the difficulties that stand in the way of man's improvement. This is enough to justify our labors.

SOLOMON FABRICANT

PART II

Reports on Selected Bureau Programs

SOME IMPLICATIONS OF THE GROWING IMPORTANCE OF THE SERVICE INDUSTRIES

"The economics of tertiary industry," wrote Colin Clark in 1940, "remains to be written. Many, as yet, feel uncomfortable about even admitting their existence." In the last twenty-five years, pioneering studies at the National Bureau by Friedman and Kuznets, Fabricant, Barger, Stigler, Kendrick, and others have done much to change that picture. Our present research, begun in the summer of 1963 with the aid of a three-year grant from the Ford Foundation, is an effort to build on this earlier work and to extend our knowledge of the service sector—defined for this study to include trade, finance, insurance and real estate, personal, professional, business, and repair services, and general government. In particular, we are attempting to measure and analyze output, input, and productivity in these industries.

Our work has been organized along three major lines. First, we have undertaken studies of individual industries, such as retail trade, state and local government, personal services, and health. Second, we have planned studies designed to shed light on problems that cut across all or most of the service industries—problems such as changes in skill mix, changes in hours, and the role of the consumer in the production process. Finally, we are attempting to view the sector as a whole and to contrast it with the rest of the economy.

This last is not to posit some bland homogeneity for all the service industries, or to deny the existence of conflicting trends within the sector. David Schwartzman's study of retailing, for instance, indicates that productivity gains have varied widely from one store type to another, and Jean Wilburn has shown that even two such apparently similar industries as barber shops and beauty parlors can behave very differently with respect to productivity. We are aware of many *intrasector* differences and intend to discuss them in various parts of the project.

In addition to such differences, however, we find that the service sector differs significantly from the rest of the economy in a number of important ways. Some of these *intersector* differences are discussed in *Productivity Trends in the Goods and Service Sectors, 1929-61: A Preliminary Survey,* Occasional Paper No. 89, published last October. Others will be developed in a second paper, "The Growing Importance of the Service Sector," which is now in preparation. My purpose here is to report a few tentative conclusions concerning the growth of services and to indicate some implications of this growth for the economy and for economic analysis.

1. THE GROWTH OF SERVICES

I begin with the observation that all of the net growth of employment in the United States in the postwar period has occurred in the service sector. As a result, this sector now accounts for more than half of total employment and more than half of gross national product. The U.S. is now a "service economy" —i.e., we are the first nation in the history of the world in which more than half of the employed population is not involved in the production of food, clothing, houses, automobiles, and other tangible goods.[1]

Although the shift of employment to the service industries has been particularly dramatic in the postwar period, it was also in evidence prior to the war, as may be seen in Table II-1 and Chart II-1.

In addition to sector comparisons, Table II-1 presents data by industry group in explicit recognition of the partly arbitrary character of the sector definitions. These definitions arise in part from our interest in a group of industries that have not received much attention in the past from economists concerned with productivity analysis. The boundary between service and goods production is very difficult to draw, and probably no division based on industrial classifications would be completely satisfactory. In practice, however, the basic point concerning the growing relative importance of services would be unaffected by any reasonable changes in definition.

Not only is there a significant difference between sector aggregates, but most individual service industries grew rapidly while most goods industries grew slowly. One-third of the goods industries experienced an absolute decline in employment between 1929 and 1963. If a service and a goods industry are chosen at random, the odds are greater than two to one that employment in the service industry will have grown faster. If we look at "service type" occupations compared with "goods type" occupations, the differential rate of growth is even greater than when the basis of classification is the industry, because service-type occupations have grown relatively, even within goods industries.

This shift of employment to services did not start in 1929. For as long as we have records on the industrial distribution of the employed population, we find a secular tendency for the percentage accounted for by the service sector to rise. Between 1870 and 1930 the differential in rates of growth averaged 1.4 per cent per annum. Since 1929 the average differential has been 1.7 per cent per annum. Between 1870 and 1920, the shift could be explained entirely by the relative decline of agriculture. Since 1920, however, the nonagricultural goods sector has not grown as rapidly as services, and in the last decade has not had any employment growth at all.

This pervasive and persistent trend has generally been attributed to sector differences in income elasticity of demand and productivity. Neither explanation can be tested precisely because accurate measures of real output are not available for many service (and some goods) industries. By making reasonable alternative assumptions about sector differentials in rates of growth of real output, however, we

---

[1] One dramatic example of this shift is that the *increase* in employment in education between 1950 and 1960 was greater than the *total* employment in primary metal industries in either year.

TABLE II-1

PERSONS ENGAGED BY SECTOR AND MAJOR INDUSTRY GROUP, SELECTED YEARS, 1929-63
(thousands)

	1929	1937	1948	1953	1957	1963
Goods	27,561	25,989	31,764	33,286	32,767	31,445
Service	18,655	21,167	26,812	31,779	33,807	37,962
Agriculture, forestry, and fishing	9,205	8,864	7,012	5,885	5,470	4,725
Mining	1,017	993	1,021	896	858	654
Construction	2,306	1,738	3,262	3,801	4,161	4,305
Manufacturing	10,556	10,686	15,468	17,462	17,054	16,767
Transportation	3,034	2,333	3,000	2,997	2,846	2,546
Communications and public utilities	1,034	901	1,281	1,403	1,514	1,461
Government enterprise	409	474	720	842	864	987
Wholesale trade	1,744	1,857	2,712	2,971	3,205	3,391
Retail trade	6,077	6,305	8,597	9,311	9,775	10,537
Finance and insurance	1,207	1,065	1,349	1,705	2,040	2,437
Real estate	368	455	574	615	681	763
Households and institutions	3,249	3,060	3,051	3,246	3,749	4,316
Professional, personal, business, and repair services	3,235	3,369	4,449	4,780	5,303	6,182
General government (including armed forces)	2,775	5,056	6,080	9,151	9,054	10,336

SOURCE: Office of Business Economics, *Survey of Current Business,* July 1964; *U.S. Income and Output, 1958; National Income, 1954 Edition.*

NOTE

Goods = Agriculture, mining, construction, manufacturing, transportation, communications and public utilities, and government enterprise.

Service = Wholesale and retail trade; finance, insurance, and real estate; services; and general government.

have formed some judgments concerning the relative importance of different explanatory factors for the period 1929-63.

1. The income elasticity of demand may have been slightly higher for services than for goods (but not higher than for goods excluding agriculture), but it is very unlikely that this was a major cause of the shift in employment. Sector differences in the rate of growth of real output were probably very small; differences in the rate of growth of real output per man were probably very large.

2. The differential in the rate of growth of real output per man probably reflects a moderate differential change in productivity in the sense of efficiency in the use of resources, but this is not the only or major explanation. It also reflects a more rapid decline in hours per man in services, a more rapid rise in the quality of labor in goods, and a more rapid rise in capital per worker in goods.

The slow growth of quality of labor and physical capital per worker can be observed in most individual service industries. An interesting instance is state and local government, where Ernest Kurnow finds that there has been no increase in capital per worker since 1929, and little change in labor skill mix.

CHART II-1

Employment, Goods and Service Sectors, 1929-40, 1946-63

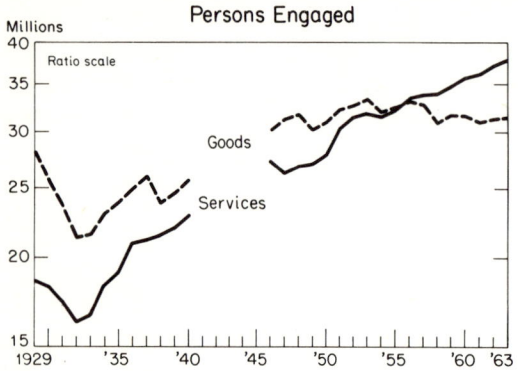

SOURCE: U.S. Department of Commerce, Office of Business Economics.
NOTE: See Table II-1 for sector definitions.

The observed differential change in capital intensity and quality of labor are in the same direction as the differential in technological change and may be complementary to it. Alternatively, they may be a response to changes in relative factor prices. Since 1929 the price of labor has tended to rise relative to the price of capital, and the price of unskilled labor has risen relative to the price of skilled labor. Such changes would have tended to alter sector employment shares because the distribution of factors was not the same in the two sectors in the initial period. Moreover, these trends were probably stronger in the goods sector than in the service sector because of the growth of unions in goods but not in services, and because many of the service industries were exempt from minimum-wage legislation.

We plan to undertake work this summer on the elasticity of substitution between skilled labor and unskilled labor and on income elasticity of demand in order to gain some insight into these questions.

2. SOME IMPLICATIONS FOR THE ECONOMY

The shift from primary to secondary production has had profound consequences for every industrial nation; the shift of employment to services may also have significant implications for the economy.

To be sure, such an attempt to look into the future is subject to important qualifications. A shift in the relative importance of different industries is only one of many changes that are occurring simultaneously in the economy, and these other changes may tend to offset the effects of interindustry shifts. Also, these shifts themselves may set in motion changes with implications different from those discussed here. Nevertheless, given the rapid growth of the service industries, it is useful to consider some of the differences between them and the rest of the economy.

LABOR

Several important sector differences in labor force characteristics are summarized in Table II-2. Probably the most significant difference is that many occupations in the service sector do not make special demands for physical strength. This means that women can compete on more nearly equal terms with men, and we find females holding down almost one-half of all service jobs compared with only one-fifth of those in the goods sector. We also find proportionately more older workers in services despite the fact that the more

TABLE II-2

LABOR FORCE CHARACTERISTICS, GOODS AND SERVICE SECTORS, 1960

Row		Percentage of U.S. Total in Goods	Percentage of U.S. Total in Service	As Percentage of Sector Employment Goods	As Percentage of Sector Employment Service
1.	All employed[a]	50	50	100	100
2.	Females	29	71	19	46
3.	Over 65	41	59	4	5
4.	Part-timers	41	59	19	27
5.	Self-employed	50	50	13	13
6.	Union members	85	15	48	7
7.	More than 12 years of school	32	68	13	30
8.	Fewer than 9 years of school	63	37	38	22

SOURCE: Rows 1-5, *U.S. Census of Population, 1960;* Row 6, H. G. Lewis, *Unionism and Relative Wages in the United States,* Chicago, 1963, p. 251; Rows 7, 8, *U.S. Census of Population, 1960,* 1/1000 sample.

NOTE: For sector definitions see note to Table II-1.

[a] Data in this table for civilian employment only.

rapidly growing sector would tend to have a younger work force.

An additional reason women and older workers are attracted to the service sector is that it provides greater opportunities for part-time employment. Trade and services, in particular, have employed large numbers of part-timers, and the number has grown appreciably in the postwar period. If data were available on those working part-time *voluntarily,* the difference between the sectors would probably be even greater than that shown in Table II-2.

The situation with respect to self-employment is complex. According to the 1960 Census of Population, the two sectors have approximately equal numbers of self-employed. Agriculture accounts for the lion's share (63 per cent) of the goods sector, while self-employment opportunities in services are widespread throughout the sector, with the exception of government and nonprofit institutions. The Census of Population undoubtedly understates the number of self-employed in services relative to goods, because corporate employees are classified as wage and salary workers, regardless of the size of the corporation. The officers of small, owner-managed corporations are, for analytical purposes, similar to partners or individual proprietors. About three-quarters of such corporations are in the service industries.

It is widely believed that opportunities for self-employment are diminishing in the United States, but if one excludes the decline of agriculture, this is no longer true. In recent years, due largely to the growth of services, the self-employed have grown absolutely and have been a constant fraction of total nonagricultural employment.[2]

The role of self-employment in the future will be determined by several conflicting

[2] See Special Labor Force Report No. 27, "Self-Employment in the United States, 1948-62," John E. Bregger, U.S. Department of Labor, Bureau of Labor Statistics, *Monthly Labor Review,* January 1963, Reprint No. 2410.

trends. A continued shift to service industry employment will tend to favor self-employment, but this may be offset by the influx of young workers and women into the labor force, since these groups are predominantly wage and salary workers. There may also be some tendency toward larger firms within each individual industry, but there is little reason to think that the door to self-employment will be closed as long as services continue to grow.

Given the importance of females, part-time employment, and self-employment in the service sector, it is not surprising to find a vast difference in the importance of unions in the two sectors. The continued growth of services may mean a decline in union influence in the United States.[3]

The last two rows of Table II-2 reveal interesting sector differences in education. The service industries make much greater use of workers with higher education, and make relatively less use of those with only limited schooling. This is not true for all service industries, of course, but it is true for the sector on average.[4]

There is another implication concerning labor which is not readily apparent in the statistics but which is potentially of considerable importance. For many decades we have been hearing that industrialization has alienated the worker from his work, that the individual has no contact with the final fruit of his labor, and that the transfer from a craft society to one of mass production has resulted in depersonalization and the loss of ancient skills and virtues.

Whatever validity such statements may have had in the past, a question arises whether they now accord with reality. The advent of a service economy may imply a reversal of these trends. Employees in many service industries are closely related to their work and often render a highly personalized service offering ample scope for the development and exercise of personal skills.

This is true of some goods-producing occupations as well, but there is little doubt that direct confrontation of consumer and worker occurs more frequently in services. Within each service industry there is some tendency for work to become less personalized (e.g., teaching machines in education, self-service counters in retailing, and laboratory tests in medicine), but with more and more people becoming engaged in service occupations the net effect for the labor force as a whole may be in the direction of the *personalization* of work.

INDUSTRIAL ORGANIZATION

The shift of employment to the service sector carries with it important implications for industrial organization in the United States because the size of the "firm" and the nature of ownership and control are typically different in the two sectors.

In goods, with some notable exceptions, such as agriculture and construction, most of the output is accounted for by large profit-seeking corporations. Ownership is frequently separate from management, and significant market power held by a few firms in each industry is not uncommon. In the service sector, on the other hand, and again with some exceptions, firms are typically small, usually owner-managed, and often noncorporate. Furthermore, nonprofit operations both public and private account for one-third of the sector's employment.

In wholesale trade, retail trade, and selected services, accounting for more than 50 per cent of the service sector, half of the employment is in companies with fewer than twenty workers. In finance, insurance, and real estate, 40 per cent is in very small firms. Another large fraction of service sector employment is accounted for by self-employed professionals and domestic servants, representing the ex-

---

[3] Cf. Leo Troy's NBER paper, *Trade Union Membership, 1897-1962,* in press.

[4] The higher *level* of education of service industry employees should not be confused with the fact that *changes* in the level of education have been greater in the goods sector.

treme in small size of employer. Even government includes many small employers. One-half of local government employment (comprising more than one-quarter of all civilian government employment) is in governmental units with fewer than 500 employees.

One statistic that epitomizes some of the trends discussed is the percentage of the national income originating in business corporations. Ever since the development of the private corporation, its role in the economy has tended to grow, but its relative importance apparently reached a peak in 1955, when corporations accounted for 55.8 per cent of total national income. Since then there has been a tendency for this fraction to decline, and in 1963 it was 53.8 per cent, approximately the same as in 1948.

Other things being equal, the shift to services tends to increase the relative importance of small firms in the economy. There are, however, forces within many industries that tend to increase the size of the average "firm." The pressure for consolidation of school districts and other local government units is a notable example. Bank mergers is another. The net effect of these countertendencies is difficult to predict.

Industries in which small firms account for the bulk of the output typically do not present industrial control problems of the "trust-busting" variety. On the other hand, there may be more need to guard against possible restrictive practices of trade associations and professional organizations. Small firms pose another problem for the economy because they may not allocate sufficient resources to research and other activities with large external benefits.

The growing importance of the nonprofit sector will probably raise some disturbing questions about how to promote efficiency and equity in such organizations. (Cf. the problems with Blue Cross.) When nonprofit operations represent only a minor exception to an essentially private-enterprise economy, the problem is not very serious; but if we ever reach the stage where nonprofit operations tend to dominate the economy, we probably will be faced with the need for radically new instruments of regulation and control.

DEMAND FOR CAPITAL GOODS

There are some portions of the service sector that use large quantities of physical capital. Real estate and the services provided by government roads and highways are notable examples. By and large, however, goods industries tend to be more capital intensive than services. In recent years (1960 through 1963) expenditures for new plant and equipment in goods industries were approximately three times as great as in profit-seeking service industries; the comparable ratio of output levels in the two groups of industries was only 1.25 to 1.00. Corporate plus noncorporate depreciation charges as a percentage of industry gross product reveal a two-to-one ratio in favor of the goods sector, and balance-sheet data from the *Statistics of Income* also suggest that capital intensity in the goods sector is roughly double that of the service sector.

In pointing out the relatively lower capital intensity of most service industries, I am not attempting to revive a "stagnation" theory in any form. The maintenance of high levels of employment and a rapid rate of growth are logically consistent with a decline in the relative importance of physical capital in the economy. The important point is to recognize that if such a decline occurs because of inter-industry shifts, it may be a proper and useful adjustment to new circumstances, with important implications for relative profit levels. While the national rate of savings may be just as high as before, other forms of investment, such as education, that are not customarily included in savings-investment estimates may take on increased importance.[5]

CYCLICAL FLUCTUATIONS

The greater stability of service industries compared with goods has been observed by Daniel Creamer in his study of *Personal Income*

---

[5]Cf. F. Thomas Juster, "Trends in Consumer Investment and Consumer Credit, 1897-1962," NBER proposed Occasional Paper, in preparation.

TABLE II-3

UNEMPLOYMENT RATES OF WAGE AND SALARY WORKERS BY
SECTOR AND INDUSTRY GROUP, 1948-63

		Average 1948-63	1948	1949	1950	1951	1952
(1)	Goods	5.8	3.9	7.3	6.1	3.4	3.0
(2)	Service	3.8	3.4	4.6	4.6	2.9	2.4
(3)	Goods excluding agriculture	5.7	3.8	7.4	5.9	3.4	3.0
(4)	Service excluding public administration	4.3	3.7	5.1	5.1	3.2	2.8
(5)	Agriculture	7.0	4.7	6.5	8.2	3.9	3.9
(6)	Mining, forestry, and fisheries	7.6	2.9	8.5	6.6	3.8	3.4
(7)	Construction	10.1	7.6	11.9	10.7	6.0	5.5
(8)	Manufacturing	5.3	3.5	7.2	5.6	3.3	2.8
(9)	Durable goods	5.3	3.4	7.4	5.2	2.6	2.4
(10)	Nondurable goods	5.3	3.6	6.9	6.0	4.0	3.3
(11)	Transportation and public utilities	3.7	3.0	5.2	4.1	1.9	1.9
(12)	Wholesale and retail trade	5.1	4.3	5.8	5.8	3.7	3.1
(13)	Finance, insurance, and real estate	2.1	1.6	1.8	2.0	1.3	1.5
(14)	Service industries	3.9	3.5	5.1	5.0	3.1	2.6
(15)	Public administration	2.1	2.0	2.9	2.8	1.6	1.1

during Business Cycles, (Princeton University Press for NBER, 1956), and by Geoffrey Moore in an unpublished study of fluctuations in employment during four postwar (1945-61) business cycles. Evidence of the greater stability of services can also be found in unemployment rates of wage and salary workers. Table II-3 presents the average rate by sector and industry group annually for 1948-63, and the average rate for the sixteen years.

We see that unemployment in goods has been consistently higher than in the service sector; the average rates over the period were 6.0 and 3.8 per cent respectively. Much of this differential can probably be explained by a greater amount of *seasonal* unemployment in goods-producing industries. The Bureau of Labor Statistics estimated that in 1957 the unemployment rates for seasonal reasons alone were as follows: agriculture 2.7 per cent, construction 4.2 per cent, manufacturing 1.5 per cent, and transportation .8 per cent, whereas in trade the rate was .6 per cent and in other private services only .3 per cent.

Of greater interest in the present context than the difference in level is the fact that unemployment in goods is more sensitive to business conditions, as may be seen in Chart II-2. The rate for each sector in each year has been plotted as an index number with the sector's average rate 1948-63 equal to 100. We note that the index for goods fluctuates more sharply than for services over the business cycle.

The larger cyclical amplitude of unemployment in goods presumably reflects larger swings in output. One of the reasons for the stability of output in services is the fact that

TABLE II-3 (concluded)

1953	1954	1955	1956	1957	1958	1959	1960	1961	1962	1963	
3.0	6.7	4.9	4.6	5.4	9.2	6.7	6.8	8.3	6.4	6.4	(1)
2.3	3.8	3.4	3.0	3.4	4.9	4.3	4.3	5.1	4.4	4.5	(2)
2.9	6.6	4.8	4.5	5.3	9.2	6.6	6.7	8.2	6.3	6.2	(3)
2.6	4.4	3.9	3.5	3.8	5.5	4.9	4.8	5.9	5.2	5.1	(4)
4.7	8.0	6.4	6.5	6.7	9.9	8.7	8.0	9.3	7.3	8.9	(5)
4.9	12.3	8.2	6.4	6.3	10.6	9.7	9.5	11.6	8.6	7.5	(6)
6.1	10.5	9.2	8.3	9.8	13.7	12.0	12.2	14.1	12.0	11.9	(7)
2.5	6.1	4.2	4.2	5.0	9.2	6.0	6.2	7.7	5.8	5.7	(8)
2.0	6.5	4.0	4.0	4.9	10.5	6.1	6.3	8.4	5.7	5.4	(9)
3.1	5.7	4.4	4.4	5.3	7.6	5.9	6.0	6.7	5.9	6.0	(10)
1.8	4.8	3.5	2.4	3.1	5.6	4.2	4.3	5.1	3.9	3.9	(11)
3.0	5.2	4.3	4.1	4.5	6.7	5.8	5.9	7.2	6.3	6.2	(12)
1.6	2.0	2.1	1.4	1.8	2.9	2.6	2.4	3.3	3.1	2.7	(13)
2.4	4.0	3.8	3.2	3.4	4.6	4.3	4.1	4.9	4.3	4.4	(14)
1.2	2.0	1.8	1.6	2.0	3.0	2.3	2.6	2.7	2.2	2.5	(15)

SOURCE: *Manpower Report of the President,* Washington, 1964, Table A-11.

the output cannot be stored. This sector, therefore, is spared the effects of swings in inventory investment, swings which make a major contribution to the cyclical fluctuations of the economy. Similarly, some service industries do not experience cyclical changes in demand comparable to the fluctuations in consumer or producer demand for durable goods. We find that cyclical swings of unemployment in nondurable goods manufacturing industries are less marked than in durable goods manufacturing; they are not as stable, however, as in services even with government excluded.

It is difficult to obtain accurate data on cyclical swings in service industry output as distinct from employment, but in my judgment the amplitude of fluctuation in output is almost certainly greater than that of employment. Thus, inferences about stability, based on employment data, should be tempered in discussing output swings.

Reasons for the discrepancy stem from the nature of the labor force in services. First, there are large numbers of self-employed; their employment is almost completely insensitive to cyclical fluctuation in output. Second, the role of salaried employees, as opposed to hourly workers, is much larger in services than it is in goods. Also, the educational level is higher and the costs of hiring are probably greater. This means that dismissals or layoffs during recessions that are expected to be short-lived will be less frequent. Finally, it should be noted that there is a substantial number of service industry employees classified as "wage and salary workers" who are actually compensated on a "piecework" basis. Their wages, in whole or in part, are determined by their output, and take the form of commissions, tips, or a share of "profits." Employers have little reason to fire such employees when business falls off. This group

CHART II-2

Annual Indexes of Unemployment Rates, Goods and Service Sectors, Relative to Their Average Rates, 1948-63

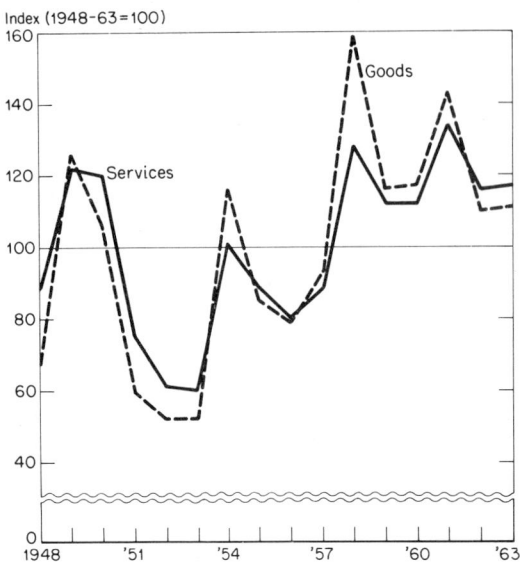

SOURCE: *Manpower Report of the President,* 1964, Table A-11.

NOTE: See Table II-1 for sector definitions.

includes real estate, insurance and security brokers, waiters and waitresses, barbers and beauticians, and most salesmen of durable goods. Because their earnings are more sensitive to cyclical fluctuations in spending than are their hours of work, we can think of these workers as having "flexible wages."[6]

3. IMPLICATIONS FOR ECONOMIC ANALYSIS

One lesson that our study of productivity in the service industries keeps forcing upon us is the importance of the consumer as a cooperating agent in the production process. To the

---

[6] I am grateful to Jacob Mincer for this formulation.

best of my knowledge, this point is neglected in the analysis of productivity in goods-producing industries, as well it might be. After all, productivity in the automobile industry is not affected by whether the ultimate drivers are bright or stupid, or whether they drive carefully or carelessly.

In services, however, the consumer frequently plays an important role in production. Sometimes, as in the barber's chair, the role is essentially passive. In such cases the only conceptual adjustment called for is to recognize that the time of the consumer is also a scarce resource. But in the supermarket the consumer actually works, and in the doctor's office the quality of the medical history the patient gives may influence significantly the productivity of the doctor. Productivity in banking is affected by whether the clerk or the customer makes out the deposit slip—and whether it is made out correctly or not. This, in turn, is likely to be a function of the education of the customer, among other factors. Productivity in education, as every teacher knows, is determined largely by what the student contributes, and, to take an extreme case, the performance of a string quartet can be affected by the audience's response. Thus, we see that productivity in many service industries is dependent in part on the knowledge, experience, and motivation of the consumer. Consider, for instance, what would happen to service industry productivity in the United States if technology and capital and labor inputs remained as they are, but the consumers were exchanged for 190 million consumers chosen at random from India.

In a similar vein, productivity can be and often is affected by the level of honesty of the consumer. If consumers can be trusted to refrain from stealing merchandise, to report prices and costs properly at check-out counters, to honor verbal commitments for purchases and other contracts, and so on, there can be tremendous savings in personnel on the part of producers of services. These savings are probably important when comparisons are made with productivity in other countries or with the same country at different points in time. It may be that qualities such as honesty are themselves functions of the general level of productivity and income. A full analysis of productivity, therefore, requires consideration of these interrelations. We expect to begin work soon on the role of the consumer in production.

Another area where the growth of services may require some refinement of concepts is in the analysis of the relation between changes in demand and changes in productivity. In many service industries it is not enough to know by *how much* demand has changed in order to predict the effect on productivity. At least two other dimensions of demand in addition to quantity must be specified.

One source of variation arises because output is frequently uneven, with peaks coming at particular hours of the day, particular days in the week, and even particular weeks in the month. During nonpeak times there is usually idle capacity. An increase in demand, if it occurs at these times, may result in very substantial gains in productivity. On the other hand, an increase in demand, if it occurs at times of peak demand, will probably not result in much or any increase in productivity.

A second source of variation is the "size of transaction," which has received some attention with respect to goods production (especially in articles by Armen Alchian and Jack Hirshleifer), but which seems to be of special importance in many service industries, such as retailing, banking, and insurance. We hope to explore this question in greater detail next year.

My final example of how the growth of services may affect economic analysis concerns the gross national product in constant dollars. This statistic is the keystone of many studies of productivity and economic growth. Unfortunately, it probably is becoming increasingly less useful for such purposes. The reason is very simple. Measures of real output in the service sector have always been unsatisfactory; as this sector becomes more important, the aggregate measure must become less satisfactory in the absence of significant improvements in the measures for individual industries.

Another trend working in the same direction is the decrease in market labor as a fraction of all time spent in productive activity. A small increase in the fraction of the adult population in the labor force has been more than offset by decreases in average hours per week and increases in vacations and holidays. Some of the increased free time may be spent in pure leisure, but probably the bulk of it is spent in the nonmarket production of goods and services and in consumer participation in the market production of services. As I have already suggested, how well or poorly these activities are carried out will surely influence economic well-being. Furthermore, both the output and inputs involved should be included in any comprehensive measure of productivity.

Economists have long been aware that the value of real GNP as a measure of economic well-being differs depending upon the level of economic development. There has been a presumption that the measure becomes more useful the more highly developed the economy is.[7]

Up to a point it is probably true that the higher the real GNP is, the more reliable it is as a measure of economic welfare. But the trend may now be in the other direction because at high levels of GNP per capita a large fraction of productivity effort will be devoted to services (where output is very difficult to measure) and to other activities that are presently not measured at all.

One aspect of the problem emerges from my study of mortality (undertaken because of our interest in the productivity of the health industry). At low and moderate levels of economic development, there is usually a negative correlation between real GNP per capita

---

[7] Cf. Simon Kuznets, "the importance of domestic activities relative to those that are part of the business system declines in the long run." *National Income and Its Composition, 1919-1938,* New York, NBER, 1941, p. 432.

and death rates. Now we have a situation where U.S. GNP per capita is 50 per cent above the Swedish level, but life expectancy is considerably lower in the U.S., and the death rate for males 50-54 is double the Swedish rate. The reasons for this huge difference are not known, but are probably related to the pace of work, diet, exercise, as well as to the productivity of the health industry.

I conclude that even as we increase our efforts to measure real output in the service sector, we must recognize that these efforts are likely to leave considerable margins of uncertainty. Future studies of growth and productivity will probably find it necessary to develop auxiliary measures of economic welfare and "output" to be used in conjunction with the gross national product.

VICTOR R. FUCHS

ON THE ACCURACY AND PROPERTIES OF SHORT-TERM ECONOMIC FORECASTS

Measure what is measurable and make measurable what is not measurable.—GALILEO GALILEI
Discontent is the first step in progress.—OSCAR WILDE

Forecasts of economic conditions aim at magnitudes that are exceedingly difficult to measure or even to define, such as the nation's aggregate output. They also often involve factors of presumed importance which are very elusive, such as the state of "business confidence." When measurement is difficult and estimates are subject to substantial errors, prediction can be particularly hazardous. Impressed also by the complexity of economic processes and the pervasiveness of chance, some would indeed question the very "predictability" of the course of economic events. This, however, misses the real point, which is that predictability is a matter of degree, and that the problem of the forecaster is to seek ways to exploit most effectively all the pertinent information available. Since this precept is easy to recognize but hard to implement, forecasters can ill afford to be perfectionists; however, in general they ought to be, and one suspects usually are, discontented with their products. If combined with a belief that it is possible to improve forecasting methods and results, the discontent is meaningful and potentially productive. It calls for systematic appraisals of the forecasts, which alone may lead to lasting improvements through a process of learning from past errors.

The need for a comprehensive and objective review of the record of their performance appears, in fact, to be generally recognized by economic forecasters of all persuasions. When the National Bureau, with the aid of a grant from several industrial companies, initiated research designed to result in such a review, it received excellent cooperation from sources of the forecasts that were to be compiled and analyzed. Work began in July 1963.

1. BACKGROUND AND SCOPE OF THE PROJECT

The primary purpose of the National Bureau study is to assess the accuracy of short-term forecasts of aggregate economic activity in the United States. This is a broad but separable category of forecasts, in which there is much general interest and which had a large share in the recent expansion of the volume and variety of economic forecasting. The restriction to "short term" means that the forecasts analyzed refer to the next year or two, or a sequence of a few shorter periods, e.g., four or six quarters. "Aggregate economic activity" refers to several different variables, all comprehensive in scope, such as the gross national product (GNP) and its major components, or the index of industrial production. Forecasts of events of special significance to the nation's economic fortunes, such as the major turning points in general business conditions, are also included. The final restriction is to authentic forecasts from reputable sources, published or unpublished, but in any case recorded before the event. The sources include individuals and small or large groups from each of three spheres that are important in generating forecasts: business, academic institutions, and government. Except for the turning-point predictions, the analysis has so far covered only forecasts stated in specific numerical terms.

In what follows, I shall report briefly on the organization of the project as a whole and at some length on that phase of it for which I am primarily responsible. But, before going into particulars, it is well to recall the general questions that were formulated at the very start of the research venture. Assuming we could assemble a sufficiently large and varied collection of authentic forecasts, and develop an adequate methodology of forecast evaluation, the following are the main substantive problems we chose to explore: How good have the forecasts been? What are the comparative merits and shortcomings of the different assumptions, techniques, and models used? To what extent and in what sense are the forecast errors systematic rather than random? What improvements are feasible to make for better and more dependable forecasts?

2. WORK IN PROGRESS

Two parts of the project are concerned mainly with the accuracy analysis of numerical forecasts. One, under my direction, deals with forecasts made without a formal specification of the underlying model or method. The other, carried on by Jon Cunnyngham, covers forecasts which have an explicit basis in econometric models, i.e., in sets of mathematical equations designed to represent the interrelations among economic variables operating over time.

The accuracy analysis results in a quantitative description of forecasting errors—their magnitudes, types, and structure. The problem is how to measure and evaluate the errors in ways that lead to meaningful inferences about the dependability and usefulness of the forecasts. Jacob Mincer's recent work on methods of forecast evaluation furthered the progress of this phase of the study.

One important factor in the forecasting process is the quality of the data inputs. Rosanne Cole is engaged in a study of the characteristics and effects of data revisions (with particular reference to GNP accounts), in addition to supervising most of the data processing for the project.

Rendigs Fels has been studying forecasters' ability to recognize turning points in the business cycle. His materials include largely qualitative forecasts, which are often difficult to interpret and evaluate because of vagueness or hedging.

Geoffrey H. Moore and Julius Shiskin have conducted research in another phase of the forecasting study, dealing with improvements in the selection and classification of business cycle indicators. They have also investigated the properties and uses of diffusion indexes with different spans.

The rest of this report will concentrate on the aggregative forecasts I have been studying. The reports of my colleagues (see Part IV) provide information on progress in the other areas of the project.

3. A SCORECARD FOR FORECAST EVALUATION

Most economic forecasts are annual and have a seasonal pattern, with a peak at year-end when predictions are made for the following calendar year. These periodic flurries of speculation about the future generate considerable excitement both within the forecasting indus-

TABLE II-4

EIGHT SETS OF ANNUAL FORECASTS OF GROSS NATIONAL PRODUCT,
INDIVIDUAL AND AVERAGE ERRORS AND COMPARISONS WITH SIMPLE EXTRAPOLATIONS, 1953-63

	\multicolumn{11}{c}{Actual Values of GNP and Errors of Forecasts in Each Year, in Billions of Dollars}	\multicolumn{2}{c}{Average Error, All Years}
	1953 (1)	1954 (2)	1955 (3)	1956 (4)	1957 (5)	1958 (6)	1959 (7)	1960 (8)	1961 (9)	1962 (10)	1963 (11)	With Regard to Sign (12)	Without Regard to Sign (13)
1. Actual GNP[a]	367.2	357.2	387.2	412.4	434.4	437.7	479.5	503.2	521.3	553.9	585.0		
2. Forecast errors,[b] set A		−10.2	−25.5	−11.4	−6.4	+1.8	−8.6	+7.7	−11.0	+9.3	−17.2	−7.2	10.9
3. B	−7.2	+8.8	−17.2	−10.4	−4.4	+11.3	−4.5	+5.8	−7.3	+12.1	−18.0	−2.8	9.7
4. C						−2.3	−9.1	+8.5	−16.3	+12.4	−12.3	−3.2	10.2
5. D				−8.7	−7.0	+1.0	−17.0	+8.6	−13.5	+0.6	−19.2	−6.9	9.4
6. E	−19.0	+2.0	−25.8	−20.1	−6.9	−4.4	−4.5	+5.3	−10.3	+4.6	−20.0	−10.4	13.4
7. F	−6.2	−5.2	−16.1	−6.4	+1.0	+4.4	+3.3	+6.8	−12.5	+11.1	−9.0	−4.8	8.1
8. G[c]	−12.0	+5.2	−9.6	−6.5	−5.4	+1.1	−16.9	+10.7	+1.8	+12.9	+8.4	+1.8	6.9
9. H		−8.7	−22.7	−12.2				+5.6	−9.0	+6.3	−15.6	−7.8	10.4
Average errors, all sets:													
10. With regard to sign	−11.1	−1.4	−19.5	−10.8	−4.8	+1.8	−8.2	+7.4	−9.8	+8.7	−12.9	−5.0	
11. Without regard to sign	11.1	6.7	19.5	10.8	5.2	3.8	9.1	7.4	10.2	8.7	15.0		9.6
12. Error in extrapolating last year's level	−19.2	+7.7	−26.7	−21.5	−19.7	+2.6	−37.8	−21.1	−16.9	−35.2	−30.3	−19.8	21.7
13. Error in extrapolating past average change	−3.6	+34.2	−14.7	−3.5	−3.8	+19.3	−23.0	−4.3	−0.1	−10.1	−11.4	−1.9	11.6

[a]First estimates by the Department of Commerce for the preceding year, which appear in February. These figures are not comparable from year to year because revisions of prior years are not entered.

[b]The annual figures for sets A, C, D, and E were in some cases obtained by averaging forecasts for the first and second half or for the four quarters of the coming year. Sets D and H are means and sets A and E are medians of a group of forecasts.

[c]These forecasts are typically made in terms of base period prices. For the purpose of these comparisons, they have been converted to current dollars, using actual prices for the forecast year. Since this eliminates the possibility of error in forecasting prices, it probably reduces the error in this set relative to the others.

try and without, among its customers and observers, but the interest in the products of all this activity typically fades away soon. Yet forecasts, to be more useful, should be treated as a crop planted at the opening of the predictive "season" (here a year) and harvested after its close, when the actual magnitudes in question can be estimated and compared with the forecasts, thus permitting appraisal of them.

In Table II-4, this treatment is applied to eight sets of forecasts of GNP for the period 1953-63. There is a column for each year covered, which starts at the top with a figure representing the "actual" level of GNP (line 1, cols. 1-11).[1] Underneath that value are listed the deviations from it of the predictions of GNP for the given year, that is, the forecast level minus actual level (lines 2-9). Below these, averages of the individual forecast errors are shown, with and without regard to sign (lines 10-11). This arrangement enables us to compare the forecasters' performance in and between any of the years. This is instructive because the state and the prospects of the economy vary from one year to another under the impact of both economic and other changes and disturbances, so that forecasters face different problems and difficulties at different times. Furthermore, forecasters communicate with one another, and the result of this communication may show up in the similarity of the errors they make.

The figures at the right end of the table summarize the record of each forecast set over the entire period covered; again, averages of the forecast errors are given here with and without regard to sign (cols. 12 and 13). Thus, reading the table line by line, one can see how a forecaster has performed in any year and compare his individual errors with those of others and with the corresponding averages. Reading down the columns, one can compare the accuracy of different forecast sources in any year and on the average over time.[2]

In addition, the table presents the errors of two simple types of extrapolation which provide common standards for screening the forecasts. The first (line 12) consists in projecting forward the last known (or estimated) value of GNP: the level of the series next year is assumed to be equal to that of this year. The second, which is far more effective (line 13), is an extrapolation of the past average change as it could have been computed from the postwar record of GNP available up to the time the forecast was made.

Table II-4 illustrates a simple and effective way of organizing basic data on forecasts. Makers and users of forecasts can readily adopt such a form to keep a running score of their own or other people's predictive successes and failures. It can suit a variety of needs by application to forecasts of different variables for different time units and periods, along with other types of summary measures of error and benchmark extrapolations. We shall use this "tableau" in the following sections to discuss, first, the over-all record of the forecasters as reflected in their average accuracy in the periods covered, and, second, the short-run variations in their performance.

The results shown in the tableau are based on eight sets of forecasts which will be used throughout this report. The forecasts represent a variety of sources and types. Four are company forecasts which are typically products of small professional teams (coded B, C, F, and G). One comes from a small group of forecasters from various industries, government, and academic institutions (set A). Another set (D) is from a group that presently

---

[1] These are early estimates which have probably more in common with the data inputs used by the forecaster than the subsequently revised figures. When the latter are used, which amounts to making the forecaster responsible for estimating the future revisions of the data, somewhat larger errors tend to be obtained. The figures in line 1 are not intended and should not be treated as a continuous annual series, because they do not give effect to the historical revisions that render them comparable.

[2] Note, however, that not all of the averages in cols. 12 and 13 relate to the same periods, which impairs their comparability.

includes about fifty business economists, for which both summary measures and forecasts by each individual participant were examined. There is a median forecast (set E) based on a poll of a large number of economists (presently about three hundred). Finally, there is a set of averages compiled from an annual summary of forecasts available since 1954 (set H). Altogether, the table records the efforts of some three or four hundred economic forecasters.[3]

4. SUMMARY MEASURES OF ERROR

Average Errors of Annual Forecasts and Extrapolations

The errors in our collection of annual forecasts of GNP averaged nearly $10 billion disregarding sign (Table II-4, line 11, col. 13). They appear small—about 2 per cent—when compared with the average level of GNP, but they are big enough to make the difference between a good and a bad business year. The average year-to-year change in GNP over the period 1953-63 amounted to about $22 billion (line 12). Thus the errors were, in terms of absolute averages, not quite one-half the size of those errors that would be produced by assuming that next year's GNP will be the same as last year's.

Furthermore, the errors of these forecasts were, on the whole, not much smaller than those which would have resulted had the forecasters simply assumed that GNP would advance next year by the average amount it had advanced in preceding years. The average error on such an assumption would have been nearly $12 billion (line 13). This exceeds the corresponding figures for all but one forecast set, but often by rather slight margins (column 13).[4]

Errors of Levels, Changes, and Base Values

The simplest measure of error is obtained by comparing the predicted and the actual levels, but it is perhaps more important to compare predicted and actual *changes*. The error in the change will be the same as that in the level, when the actual level at the time of the forecast is known. As a rule, however, this is not so and the two will differ by the amount of error in the estimated current position, which is the base of the forecast.

The errors in the estimated current position are, of course, typically smaller than the errors in forecasts proper, since the present is generally better known than the future. However, they are by no means negligible. They average about one-fourth or one-third of the corresponding errors of the level forecasts for GNP, and from 12 to 50 per cent for industrial production.

For GNP, the errors of change forecasts tend to be smaller than those of level forecasts. The latter, as shown in Table II-4, average about $10 billion when taken without regard to sign; the former average about $9 billion, or 10 per cent less. For industrial production, there is less regularity in the relation between the level and the change forecasts because errors of base and of level often differ in sign.

Chart II-3 compares the actual year-to-year changes in GNP and industrial production with the changes forecast by one of the better, but not unrepresentative, forecast records. Clearly the pattern of predicted changes is broadly similar to that of the actual changes. This is true of each of the eight forecast sets examined here.[5]

---

[3] Some forecasters may be in more than one group.

[4] An extrapolation of the average historical change produces in effect good trend estimates for series that tend to grow smoothly, such as postwar GNP. Such extrapolations prove then to be a rather severe, if simple, yardstick. They would be less adequate for economic magnitudes that fluctuate more widely, such as unemployment.

[5] The significance of this relation will be better appreciated when compared with the definitely inferior results obtained for extrapolations. Thus the use of the average historical change, as described above, produces relatively good projections for GNP, in terms of the over-all average errors, but predicted change here is nearly constant from one year to the next. Graphically, it would approximate a straight line cutting through the "actual" GNP changes in Chart II-3 at the $20 billion level.

CHART II-3

Actual and Predicted Changes and Errors, Gross National Product and Industrial Production, 1953-63

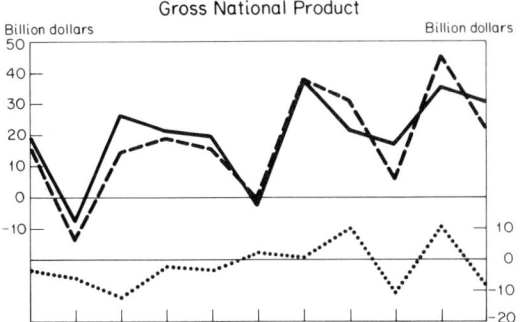

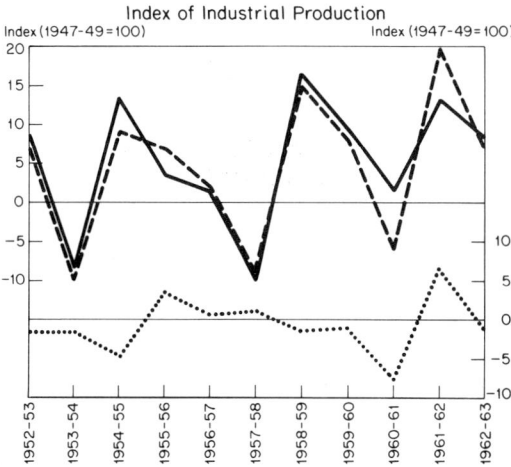

NOTE: Actual changes are based on first estimates published by the source after the end of the forecast year.

Underneath the paired curves for changes, Chart II-3 shows the discrepancies between them, i.e., the errors of the change forecasts. These are on the whole much smaller than the corresponding changes themselves: as already noted, the forecasts are typically better than simple extrapolations of last year's level, which assume no change and therefore produce errors equal to the actual changes.

It should not be inferred from this chart that changes in GNP and industrial production are effectively forecast a full year ahead. As noted below, our records of quarterly forecasts suggest that forecasters typically achieve a considerable measure of success in forecasting the next one or two quarters, but limited success beyond that. The annual record can likewise be interpreted as implying an effective forecasting range of no more than two quarters. Not only are the forecasts typically made late in the preceding calendar year, but a record of accuracy very similar to that shown here could be attained merely by accurately forecasting the first two quarters of the ensuing year and assuming no change beyond that.

THE UNDERESTIMATION BIAS

The tendency of forecasters to underestimate changes, which has been observed elsewhere,[6] is evident in most of our data. Thus the mean changes in actual values exceed those in predicted values for all but one of the forecast sets examined; the actual changes in GNP average about $22 billion and the predicted changes $19 billion.

When underestimation applies to increases in the predicted series, then the future levels of the series will also as a rule be underestimated. (This follows necessarily if the current position is known or itself understated.) On the other hand, underestimation of decreases would tend to result in overestimation of levels. In series with upward trends, such as GNP or industrial production, increases are more frequent than decreases, so that the levels are understated most of the time. (Note that all but one of the average errors in Table II-4, col. 12, are negative.)

However, in the GNP forecasts it is primarily the increases that were underestimated, not the decreases. Recent recessions have been sufficiently mild and short to cause only very small declines, or even merely retardations of growth, in the *annual* values of GNP. According to early estimates, declines occurred in

---

[6]H. Theil, *Economic Forecasts and Policy*, Amsterdam, 1958, Chaps. III-V.

1953-54 and 1957-58.[7] On the former occasion, most forecasts showed larger declines than actually occurred; and on the latter, most of them missed the downturn. In the years when GNP increased, on the other hand, underestimates were almost twice as frequent as overestimates. Industrial production declined much more in the recessions than did GNP, and its contractions were in fact underestimated by most forecasters (though a few greatly overestimated the drop in output in 1954).

If underestimation of changes was merely the result of failure to forecast irregular or random variations in the actual values, it would not constitute an error or "bias" that forecasters could or should guard against. Forecasting errors that can be traced directly to short random movements must be regarded as unavoidable: a sudden outbreak of war or a strike started without warning can hardly be events that an economic forecaster should be expected to predict (though his job certainly does include an evaluation of the effects of such events, once known, on the course of the economy). To put it differently, in principle the requirement of a good forecast is that it predict well the systematic movements of the given variable—not that it predict perfectly the actual values of the latter. It could not do that, except by accident, for economic series where random elements are virtually always present.

However, the observed underestimation is, in fact, partly systematic. This is indicated by the strong prevalence of negative signs among the errors of predicted changes: the means of the change forecasts are, with few exceptions, smaller than the means of the actual changes.[8]

---

[7]Subsequent revisions reduced the decline of GNP in 1953-54 and converted the small decline in 1957-58 into a very small increase.

[8]Smoothing out the irregular movements would simply tend to make the *variance* of predicted changes less than that of actual changes; averages of predicted and of actual changes, taken with regard to sign, should not be systematically different.

Also, there is direct evidence that not only the erratic changes but also the systematic cyclical movements in comprehensive economic aggregates are typically underestimated (see Table II-5, below).

LARGER ERRORS OF LONGER-SPAN FORECASTS

Five of our forecast sets provide chains of predictions made at a given date for two or more successive periods, e.g., for the first and second half, or the four quarters, of the coming year. These data have been used to analyze the performance of forecasts over different intervals between the current base and the future target (which we call the *span* of the forecast).

The evidence shows clearly that the accuracy of short-term forecasts diminishes as the span increases. Both levels and changes are predicted better over the next three months than over the next six, and better over six months than over nine or twelve. Only a few examples of this highly regular and pervasive relation can be given here, but they are representative and telling. In a semiannual forecast of GNP for 1955-63 by a rather large group of business economists, the mean absolute errors of change are, for a six-month span, $6.7 billion; for a twelve-month span, $12.3 billion. In a quarterly forecast by the staff of a large company for the same years, the average errors, in billions of dollars, are for one quarter 5.0, for two quarters 8.4, for three, four, five, and six quarters 11.9, 13.7, 15.5, and 17.1, respectively. Again, in a semiannual forecast of the Federal Reserve Index of Industrial Production for 1947-63, the mean absolute errors are 3.6 index points (1947-49=100) for six, and 7.1 points for twelve months. Similar progressions in the size of errors appear also in forecasts of other variables, such as the components of GNP.

In general, extrapolations of various types also tend to worsen with the lengthening of the predictive span. Since many forecasters use such extrapolative techniques, this is presumably a part of the explanation for the observed association between longer forecasts and larger errors. Other ingredients of forecasts—variables that typically move in advance of the predicted series, anticipations data, and the forecaster's own judgment—also are probably decreasingly reliable over longer spans, hence contribution to the deterioration of the resulting forecast.

While the annual and shorter forecasts are generally superior to extrapolations, those with longer spans (say of twelve to eighteen months) are often worse than the more effective types of extrapolation, including projections of the average historical change as used in Table II-4.

5. SHORT-RUN VARIATIONS IN FORECASTERS' PERFORMANCE

Year-to-Year Comparisons of Forecasting Errors

It is often said that forecasters have their "off years"—periods in which they generally go wrong because of some difficulties inherent in the type of economic change that occurred at that time. In other periods, it is believed, no such special difficulties exist, and forecasters tend to be "right."

A year-by-year survey of forecasters' performance will help appraise this view and its implications. Our records show that the increases in both GNP and industrial production were underestimated most in the boom year 1955. Consequently, the level of economic activity was also underestimated most in that year (Table II-4, line 10). Errors of the same kind were made also in 1961, following the latest recession, and in 1963, when the economy showed unexpected vigor after a retardation. On the other hand, in the recession years 1958 and 1960, the predicted levels of GNP and industrial production were too high, either because the changes were understated or because no declines were expected. The retardation of 1962 was widely missed, with the result that the forecast levels were again too high. Finally, the 1954 recession, as already noted, turned out to be milder than many forecasters apparently anticipated, particularly in terms of GNP.

It should be noted that the timing of recent business cycle downturns was early enough to make the presence of the recession rather generally known by the end of the peak year (1953, 1957, and 1960). This, plus the presumption that the contractions would continue to be short, made the task of predicting annual changes relatively easy.

Another fact, illustrated in Chart II-3, is the correspondence between the year-to-year changes in the mean forecast errors of GNP and in those of industrial production. The patterns of changes have actually been quite similar in the two variables, and the forecasts we have reviewed reflect this similarity.

Forecasting and Business Cycles

The year-to-year comparisons of the preceding section suggest that predictive errors are affected by the cyclical characteristics of the forecast period. Table II-5, which utilizes forecasts for quarters and half-years, demonstrates this still more clearly. The levels of GNP and industrial production are underestimated most in the first year of expansion, when the increases in these series are very large. Later in the expansion, when the increases are usually smaller, the levels are underestimated much less; and they may even be overestimated, as happened in the "retardation" of 1962. In contractions, overestimation of levels is the rule, sometimes because the downturn is missed and sometimes because the decline turns out to be larger than predicted.

To understand how such results might come about, it may be helpful to distinguish two predictive patterns, both of which would underestimate current cyclical changes, though in very different ways. First, imagine a series of forecasts which traces the fluctuations in the actual series, but with a short lag. The observed cyclical amplitudes need not be underestimated, but the current changes at certain stages of the cycle will be. Second, imagine a series of forecasts which faithfully reproduces the trend, but not the cyclical movements, of

TABLE II-5

AVERAGE ERRORS IN FORECASTS OF GNP AND INDUSTRIAL PRODUCTION DURING
THREE STAGES OF BUSINESS CYCLES, 1947-63

CODE OF FORECAST AND PERIOD COVERED	Variable Predicted and Unit	MEAN ERROR IN FORECAST LEVEL DURING		
		First Year of Expansion	Rest of Expansion	Contraction
A—1948, 1955-63	GNP ($ billion)[a]	−19.2	−4.4	+1.0
C—1958-62	GNP ($ billion)[b]	−14.0	+2.9	+4.6
D—1947-62	Indus. prod. (1947-49=100)[c]	− 7.1	−4.4	+3.2

[a] Forecasts for the first and second half of the coming year.

[b] Forecasts made quarterly for sequences of up to five quarters ahead.

[c] Forecasts made twice in the year for two or three semiannual periods ahead. The forecasts for the eighteen-month spans cover the period from 1948 through the first half of 1956.

the actual values. The predictions simply cut across the fluctuations, so that here both the cyclical amplitudes and the current short-period changes are underestimated.

Some forecasts look more like the lagging cyclical model, others the trend-projection model. In Chart II-4, the former is illustrated by forecast C, and the latter by forecast G, for GNP during 1958-61. Both these sets consist of forecasts made for several quarters ahead, which in the chart are linked together into chains that fan out to the right from points representing the forecasters' estimates of the current position. The forecasts are made twice or four times a year, and hence the chains overlap. The C chains have "kinks" in 1958 and 1960-61, which lag the turning points in GNP; the G chains show no kinks at all.

Forecasts of the trend-projection type, such as G, come out rather well in terms of measures of average errors, largely because they are relatively optimistic and avoid the large underestimation bias of the "cyclical" forecasts. It is clear, however, that forecasts such as these must be regarded as failures with respect to the recognition of turning points. The chain forecasts with cyclical patterns can be more useful in this role, even when they are tardy.

6. USES OF FORECAST EVALUATIONS

The services that forecasts are expected to render depend on the needs of the user and are not easily defined by an outside observer. Surely, however, the usefulness of a forecast is in the first instance a function of its accuracy. With the growth of public interest in the expanding activity of economic forecasting, there is increasing need for objective and comprehensive evaluations of forecasting accuracy— a need as yet largely unsatisfied. Our study will help to fill it by working out and applying systematic methods of testing short-term economic predictions.

Makers of forecasts, as well as users, have a vital interest in a review of their record of performance. Let me give two examples of

CHART II-4

Two Sets of Chain Forecasts of GNP for 1958-61 and the Corresponding Actual Values

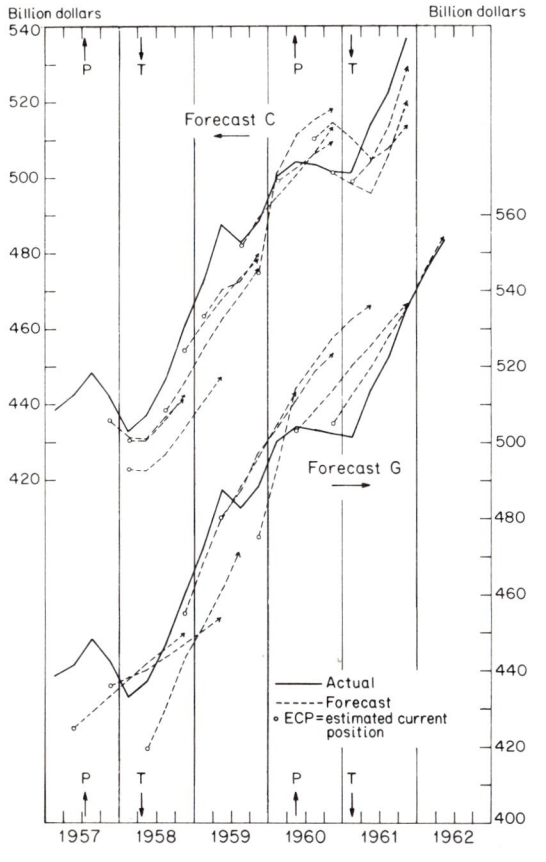

NOTE: P and T represent business cycle peaks and troughs, respectively.

simple improvements in forecasting methods and results that have so far been suggested by our study. First, we have found a great deficiency in forecasters' records of the current position at the time of forecast. These records are essential to a proper appraisal. Second, better utilization of the historical content of the series is also needed. It seems desirable that, at some stage, trend projections should be incorporated in the forecasting process, since our study shows that many forecasts looking ahead four quarters or more are inferior to simple trend extrapolations. As our work proceeds, we expect that advantages and disadvantages of different forecasting techniques will come increasingly to the surface.

The general economist, finally, can benefit from a study of the properties of forecasts, since they throw light upon the formation and revisions of economic expectations. With this in mind, we are giving considerable attention to forecasts of chains of short periods that partially overlap in time, since such materials are particularly informative here. Also, our study reveals a large degree of interdependence, though often a wide dispersion, among forecasts made at a particular time (cf. Table II-4). This has important implications for theories of economic change.

VICTOR ZARNOWITZ

CONSUMER CREDIT MARKETS: A PROGRESS REPORT

The current consumer credit study reflects the National Bureau's continued interest in this segment of the credit market. Until the first Studies in Consumer Instalment Financing were published by the Bureau in the 1930's, little was known about the nature and operations of institutions serving the consumer's credit needs, only scattered statistical estimates measuring the volume of credit existed, and little had been done to ascertain the risks and costs inherent in consumer credit operations. Since the 1930's, consumer credit has grown enormously in absolute and in relative terms. The present study was designed to reexamine some of the results of the earlier study in the light of the additional experience and statistical data available; to extend the research into subjects, such as rates of charge, which had been treated sparingly if at all; and to assess the significance of consumer credit developments in the changed economic circumstances of today.[1]

The work on the individual studies has begun to produce tentative answers to various questions.[2] How rapidly have consumer credit markets grown in importance to the national economy? How do these markets function? What rate and cost relations exist among the institutions serving consumers? What is the nature of the demand for consumer instalment credit? Do consumers know the levels of rates of charge and can they discern differences in rates of charge? What kinds of credit information are given consumers and what procedures are necessary to make them comparable? Where do the funds lent to consumers originate and are these sources affected by changing monetary conditions? Finally, does access to consumer credit play a stabilizing or destabilizing role when unemployment occurs?

CONSUMER CREDIT AND THE NATIONAL ECONOMY

F. Thomas Juster's preliminary findings on trends in consumer investment and consumer credit between 1897 and 1962 indicate that instalment credit has become increasingly important to the national economy through its contribution to the rapid growth of the stock of capital owned by consumers—automobiles, kitchen appliances, and so forth. Chart II-5 shows the rapid rate of growth of two forms of household capital (dwellings and major durable goods), and also indicates that both long-term mortgage debt and short-term instalment debt grew even more rapidly. The implication is clear that the household sector has increasingly relied upon credit to finance a growing stock of consumer capital.

Juster points out that gross additions to consumer capital have been a rising fraction of gross national product, while gross additions to capital owned by business enterprise have been a declining fraction (Chart II-6). These differential trends necessarily imply a shift in the composition of gross fixed capital formation. In the decade from 1899 to 1908, his figures show, business enterprises accounted for roughly two-thirds of gross fixed capital formation, households for about one-quarter, and government for about one-tenth. By 1949-58, the share of the enterprise sector had declined to about 40 per cent of the total, the household sector accounted for nearly one-half, and the government share had risen to 15 per cent (excluding military capital expenditures). Gross capital formation is now larger in the household than in the enterprise sector.[3]

The relative contribution of the household and enterprise sectors to cyclical fluctuations in capital goods output has changed as well. From the turn of the century to the beginning of the First World War, short-run variations in the output of capital goods purchased by business enterprises were four to five times as great (in dollar magnitude) as those in consumer capital formation. In the post-World War II period, the variations in output of capital goods purchased by households were 50 per cent larger than the corresponding fluctuations for the enterprise sector.

Marked changes in credit markets and financial institutions have accompanied these structural changes in the nature and composition of capital formation. There has been an almost uninterrupted liberalization of the credit terms made available to consumer borrowers as the market came to embrace larger and larger segments of the population. Although the rates

---

[1] The current study was made possible by grants from four large sales finance companies. We have benefited from the assistance of an advisory committee under the chairmanship of Paul W. McCracken, University of Michigan.

[2] At the present time one book and four Occasional Papers have been published, a second book and fifth Occasional Paper are in press, and four other reports are in preparation. For a list of these reports and further detail on the studies in progress, see Part IV, section 4.

[3] It does not necessarily follow that net capital formation is also larger in the household sector.

CHART II-5

Major Types of Household Tangible Assets and Related Debt, 1897-1962

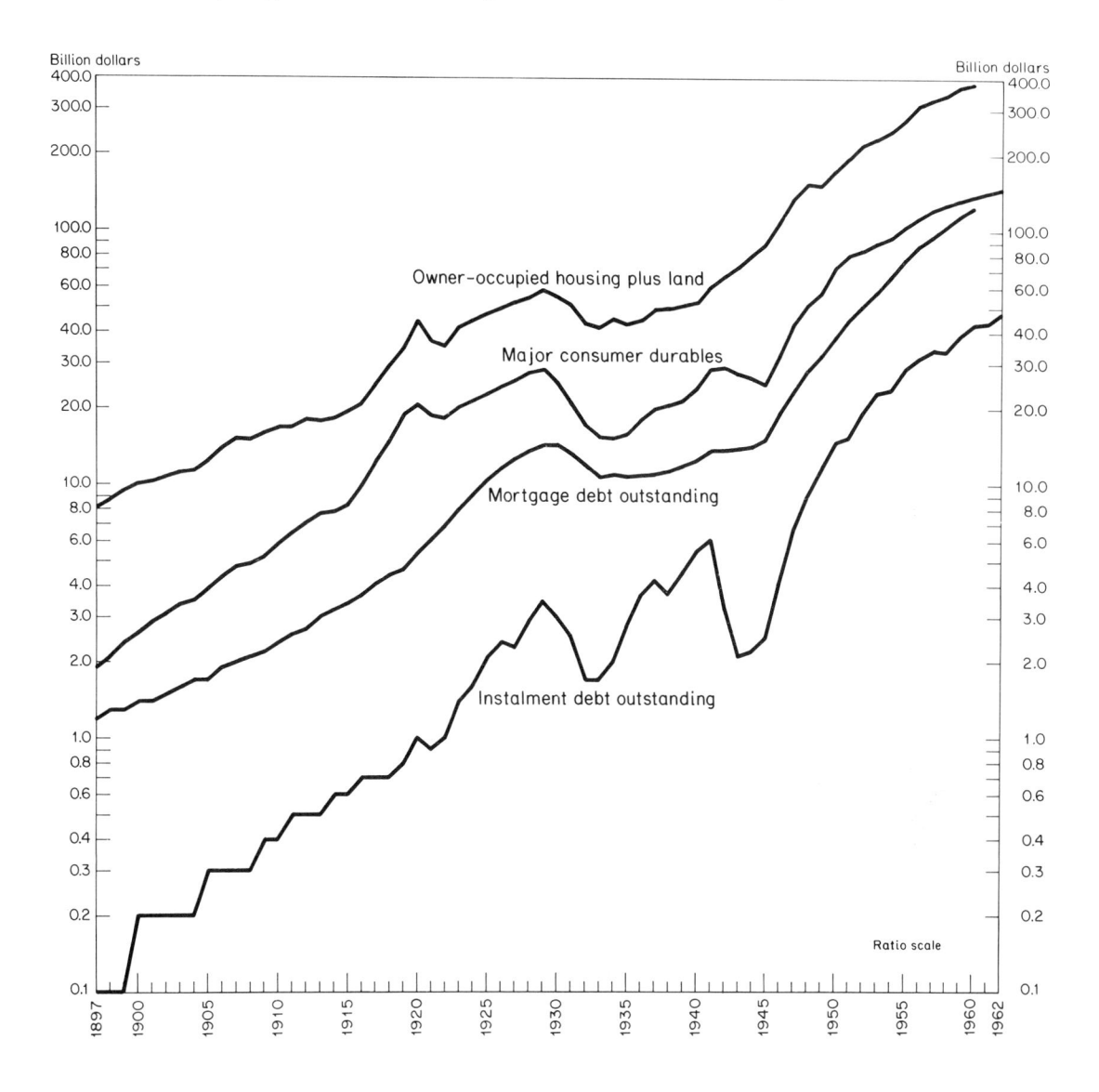

SOURCE: F. Thomas Juster, "Trends in Consumer Investment and Consumer Credit, 1897-1962," NBER, in preparation.

of charge on consumer debt have apparently declined over the decades (see below), our studies suggest that the change in credit terms, rather than lower finance rates, was the more important element in the rise in borrowing.

THE FUNCTIONING OF THE AUTOMOBILE CREDIT MARKET

A large portion of our investigation of how consumer credit markets function has been devoted to the automobile market, partly because

CHART II-6

Gross Investment by Households and Business Enterprises, 1897-1963

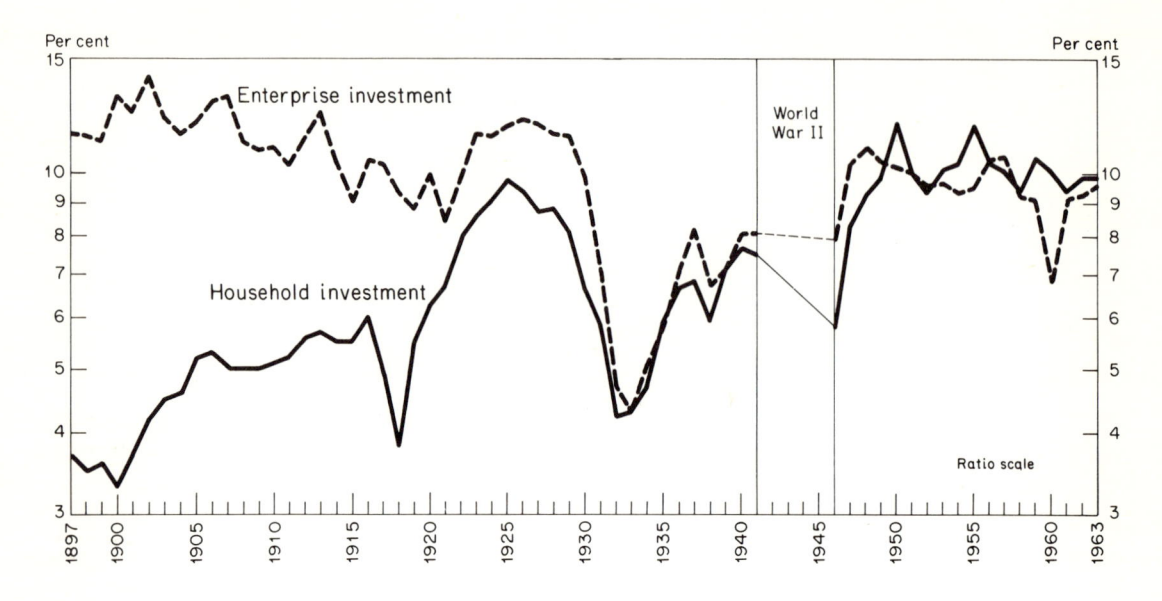

SOURCE: Same as Chart II-5; 1963 estimated.

of its importance and partly because data concerning the price of credit, which we defined as the finance rates, were more readily available here. A first step was to construct estimates of finance rates on automobile credit contracts. Three large samples of sales finance company contracts with reasonable geographic coverage were used as benchmarks, covering 1935-38, 1954-55, and 1958-59. My portion of the work was to construct time series estimates of finance rates and to analyze factors affecting rate levels. Wallace P. Mors, using the same data, has studied the effects of state legal rate ceilings upon finance rates.

We were surprised by the variation in new-auto finance rates over time. Rates apparently declined from levels approximating 15 per cent in the 1920's to about 11 per cent in the early 1950's, then rose to about 12.5 per cent in 1960.[4] Since then, sales finance company new-auto rates have declined more than a full percentage point, a greater decline that that observable in residential mortgage rates (Chart II-7). The recent decline in finance rates and mortgage rates in relation to other borrowing rates may reflect the increased flows of funds into savings accounts in commercial banks and thrift institutions. This, along with other factors, appears to have increased rate competition among banks and sales finance companies for automobile credit and lowered finance rates.

The automobile credit market is patronized by borrowers who either finance their obligations through dealers or obtain loans directly from lending agencies. Commercial banks make loans directly and purchase paper through dealers. As a result, three major types of credit sources can be distinguished: sales finance companies (which purchase dealer paper), indirect financing banks, and direct lending banks. The 1954-55 sample of credit contracts provided us with an opportunity to compare factors affecting rates among these sources. The factors that appear to be most significantly related to the level of finance rates

---

[4] The finance rate series is presented in Part IV, section 4.

CHART II-7

New-Auto Finance Rates, Home First-Mortgage Rates, and Bank Rates on Business Loans, 1924-64

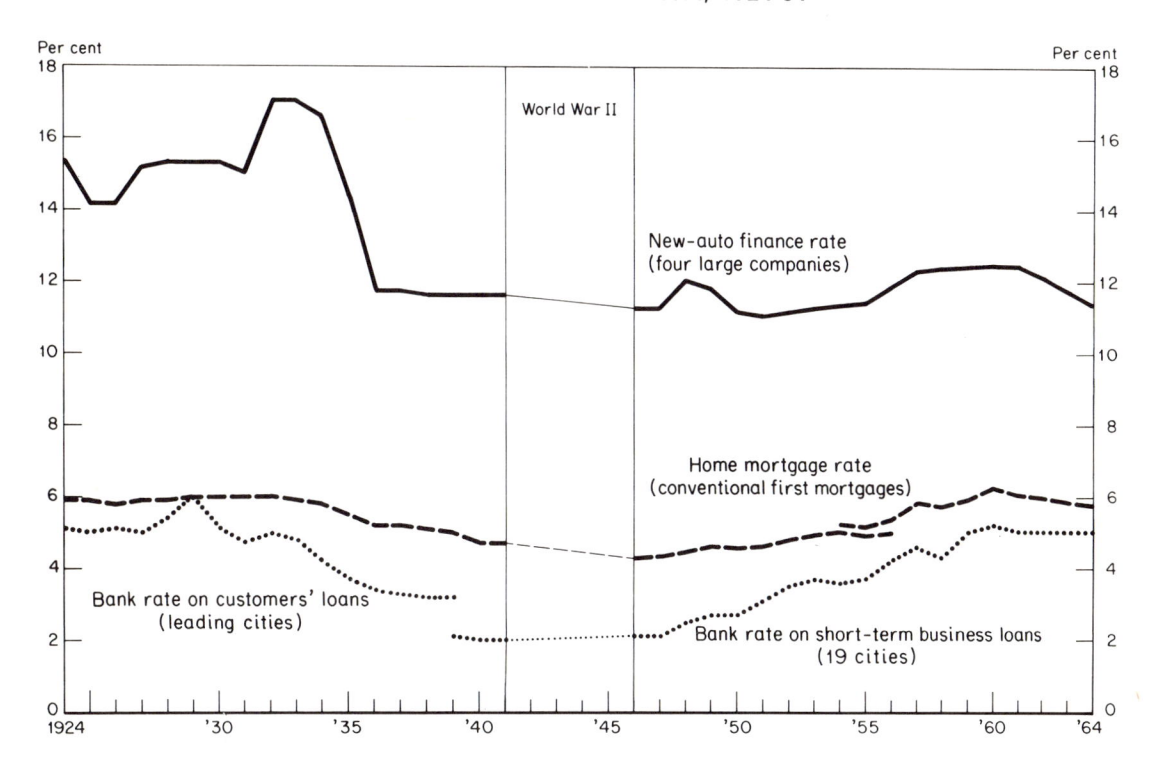

SOURCE: Finance rate series from Robert P. Shay, *New-Automobile Finance Rates, 1924-62,* New York, NBER, 1963, Table 8, with minor revisions; mortgage rate series: 1924-56, Saul B. Klaman, *The Postwar Residential Mortgage Market,* Princeton for NBER, 1961, Table A-6; 1954-62, FHA; 1963-64, new homes only, HLBB in cooperation with FDIC, *Federal Reserve Bulletin,* February, 1965; and business loan rates for 1924-28 from Winfield W. Riefler, *Money Rates and Money Markets in the United States,* New York, 1930, and *Federal Reserve Bulletins* for the years thereafter.

NOTE: With the greater prevalence of second and third mortgages in the earlier years, home mortgage borrowing costs probably declined over the period. All of the three series shown above reflect nominal rates and are not adjusted for fees, product prices, and compensating balances. The 1939 data for business loan rates are overlapped; the higher rate is a two-month average and the lower rate is a ten-month average from the revised series.

are type of credit source, size of city, legal rate ceiling, dealer's markup over factory price of auto, purchase of credit life insurance, and borrower's occupation. For the market as a whole, it appears that elements of the credit contract itself, legal restraints, and institutional differences among credit sources are of primary importance to rate levels.

Wallace Mors's study of the effects of legal ceilings upon finance rates and the dealer's share of the rate provides important additional insights into the automobile credit market. Mors finds, in his investigation of the 1958-59 sample of sales finance contracts for both new and used automobiles, that consumer rates are generally well below ceiling, indicating that competitive forces are operative. He also finds that legal rate ceilings exert some influence upon the level of finance rates charged borrowers.

Although these matters are still under study, the results so far suggest the following observa-

29

tions about the functioning of the automobile credit market. First, active price competition among sellers of credit has resulted in variations in finance rates over time and kept rates well below legal ceilings. Second, the pairing of buyers and sellers according to the price of credit does not appear to be governed directly by the creditworthiness of the individual borrower, but rather by differentiating elements in credit contracts, legal restraints, and general institutional policies. On balance these factors seem to result in a reasonable sorting of credit customers according to risk, that is, in a manner consistent with rate of charge.

INSTITUTIONAL COSTS OF PROVIDING CREDIT

While the analysis of the automobile credit market suggests that competition among sellers of credit exercises a large influence upon finance rates, the relation between income and expenses among the institutions providing credit also is indicative of the extent to which consumers receive protection through the operation of competitive forces under existing legal constraints. Paul F. Smith's book, *Consumer Credit Costs, 1949-59,* revealed that the costs of providing consumer credit are generally high in comparison with other kinds of credit, and that net profit rates are broadly comparable with those in manufacturing industries.

Operating expenses among four types of institutions studied (consumer finance companies, sales finance companies, commercial banks, and credit unions) were extremely wide, ranging from $14.25 to $3.30 per hundred dollars of outstanding credit in 1959. Many factors contribute to the level and to variations in costs. The method of acquiring business, differences in character of risks assumed, variations in size of credit contracts, legal controls upon operating practices, and some implicit costs inherent in credit union operations all contributed to the wide range in recorded costs. During 1949-59 the spread in average rates among the four types of institutions declined, a development that seems attributable both to competitive factors and to a narrowing of the differences among the kinds of consumer loan services provided to borrowers.

THE DEMAND FOR CONSUMER INSTALMENT CREDIT

Even if rate competition exists and if profits are at competitive levels, it does not necessarily follow that credit markets function perfectly. In *Consumer Sensitivity to Finance Rates,* F. Thomas Juster and I undertook an experimental questionnaire sampling of Consumers Union subscribers to test the hypothesis that the market for consumer instalment credit is imperfect—in the sense that the bulk of consumer borrowers are "rationed" with respect to the amounts of credit they can obtain at going rates of charge. Because of institutional limits upon rates, down payments, maturities, and loan sizes, we believe that most consumers accumulate more equity than they desire when purchasing durable goods instalment credit. As a result, they are insensitive to finance rates because they value equity funds more than the marginal costs of borrowing in the market. Borrowers in these circumstances are strongly impelled to obtain the largest amount of credit available—usually associated with the longest maturity and lowest monthly payment.

Our data are consistent with the hypothesis that there are substantial differences in rate elasticity between groups of borrowers classed as "rationed" and "unrationed." The former group included younger married families and those with small liquid asset holdings and a relatively favorable attitude toward credit use. The rate elasticity of this group was virtually nil. On the other hand, in the unrationed group —older married families or single persons with higher incomes and liquid assets, and those with an unfavorable attitude toward credit use —rate elasticity was considerably higher. Since the majority of consumer borrowers probably fall in the rationed category, our results suggest that little rate sensitivity would be observable in the population as a whole.

In this same work, Juster and I attempted to ascertain the extent of consumer knowledge of finance rates actually paid on recently financed durable goods purchases. The majority of borrowers, some 82 per cent, were unable to give rates estimates of reasonable accuracy. Yet respondents did seem to know that certain types of credit were more expensive than others. They knew, for example, that automobile loans were less costly than furniture loans and that small loans were more expensive than large loans. We termed this "institutional" knowledge because other research has suggested that borrowers may draw such broad distinctions by associating high and low rates with particular types of institutions.

RATE INFORMATION AND QUOTATION

Wallace P. Mors's book, *Consumer Credit Finance Charges: Rate Information and Quotation*, now in press, traces the origins and development of the various forms in which consumers receive finance charge information, reviews the procedures they must follow to make comparisons among credit alternatives, and evaluates the extent to which the variety of information given can be used by consumers to make effective comparisons of credit cost. Mors's major conclusion is that no single method of quoting charges, whether in dollars or rates of charge, is a reliable guide to credit cost, taken by itself. Among the several forms of information—monthly payment size, effective monthly or annual rates, add-on or discount rates on the amount borrowed—each may serve as a useful guide to credit cost in certain situations but have little value in others. Mors notes problems confronting consumers in using the varied information effectively and concludes that the diversity of state legislation contributes to the lack of uniformity encountered among the systems used to compute and quote charges.

In this connection it is of interest to note that the National Conference of Commissioners on Uniform State Laws has established a project for the purpose of drafting comprehensive uniform or model state legislation to govern consumer credit. Members of their staff have shown considerable interest in our reports and have stated that they have found them useful for their purposes.

SOURCES OF FUNDS FOR CONSUMER CREDIT

Richard T. Selden, in Occasional Paper 85, *Trends and Cycles in the Commercial Paper Market*, explored the rapid resurgence of this market in the postwar period. He found that the demand for commercial paper funds was determined by the amount of receivables which finance companies could acquire profitably and by the relative cost of commerical paper and bank loans. The supply of funds appeared to be quite elastic with respect to the differential between paper yields and Treasury-bill yields. Both demand and supply were sensitive to cyclical conditions. The divergent cyclical behavior of the volume of directly placed paper compared with that of dealer paper—the former rising and falling with the business cycle and the latter showing countercyclical movements—is a major finding which Selden explains in terms of differential demand and supply hypotheses. Selden's remaining work on sources of funds to the finance industry is still in preparation.

FINANCIAL ADJUSTMENTS TO UNEMPLOYMENT

In an Occasional Paper now in press, Philip A. Klein analyzes the financial adjustments to unemployment made by families receiving unemployment compensation, in order to determine how and to what extent consumer credit affects these adjustments. Working with questionnaires originated by the Department of Labor in six field surveys between 1954 and 1958, the study ascertains the manner in which these families were able to adjust to the loss of income when unemployment occurred. Unemployment compensation was the major source of funds to offset the decline in income, reducing the gross loss in family earnings by

32 per cent. To offset the drop in family income net of unemployment compensation, families reduced their net worth to the extent of 34 per cent of the income decline and reduced consumption expenditures the remaining 66 per cent. Reductions in liquid asset holdings accounted for two-thirds of the net worth reduction, and debt adjustments accounted for the remaining third. Debt adjustments took the form of borrowing from friends, relatives, or financial institutions, running up unpaid bills, or allowing delinquencies and repossessions to occur on instalment obligations. While impairment of net worth has long-run consequences for those who suffer unemployment, Klein points out that in the short run it does permit a less drastic cut in consumption expenditures and cushions the aggregate effects of unemployment upon the rest of the economy. Klein also found that the longer unemployment lasted, the greater was the reduction in consumption expenditures, since resources get used up and other adjustments in net worth become more difficult to make. He concludes that unemployment compensation, the liquidation of assets, and adjustments in debt position all acted as stabilizing influences, although unemployment compensation has far greater quantitative importance and has the advantage of not impairing the net worth of unemployed families.

SUMMARY REPORT

A summary report on the study's major findings is being prepared. It will review trends and cycles in credit; compare the relative importance of the several institutions supplying credit; discuss the effects of changes in rates, terms, and sources of funds; and, finally, assess the contribution of consumer instalment credit to the nation's economic performance.

ROBERT P. SHAY

PART III

Studies New and Completed

NEW STUDIES

One of the most difficult yet important problems of our time is whether, or to what degree, trends in the price level are related to the rate of advance of a nation's prosperity. The problem is usually put in more specific terms, as follows: whether, and if so how, a free society can achieve significant increases in productivity, reach and maintain reasonably full employment, and yet avoid inflation. The National Bureau, with the aid of a five-year grant from the Alfred P. Sloan Foundation, has decided to embark upon a program of studies bearing on this problem.

Plans for such a program are being developed along three lines. First, a statistical review would be undertaken to provide a tolerably solid basis for economic analysis, as well as for improving current guides to economic policy. This would attempt to draw on existing materials for the United States covering the past fifty years or more and for Western Europe and Japan in recent decades, but some new factual investigations will also be required. Among those that promise useful results are efforts to account for developments in the role of the family and governmental sectors, not now adequately covered in our national income accounts; to explore possible biases in price indexes; and to reappraise critically the validity of employment and unemployment statistics for the United States, especially prior to 1940.

A second area of research would embrace historical studies: first, of the relations between general price trends and prosperity in various periods and countries; and second, of the relations between the behavior of relative prices, wages, employment, and production, on the one hand, and productivity trends, on the other, in individual industries in the United States. Especially interesting is the recent period of relative price stability in the United States, which should be studied against the background of other periods of price stability here and abroad as well as periods when upward or downward trends predominated.

A third area of research would be concerned with analyses of policies for promoting prosperity without inflation. Of large interest would be a study, both empirical and analytical, of wage and price policies—including of course the so-called wage and price "guidelines"—in the context of the present economic setting in the United States. Also important would be a study of lags in the implementation of monetary and fiscal policies—lags that arise from delays in recognizing the need for change in policy, from delays in taking action once it appears that action is needed, and from delays between action taken and the response. The need for such a study is indicated by the fact that current differences about the desirable course of monetary policy are traceable, in very large part, to differences of judgment about the length of these lags. Of course, in order to understand better the changing environment within which decisions on policy have to be made, it would be useful at least to survey—from the viewpoint of policy action—the developments, both normal and distinctive, that unfold in the course of business cycles.

The problem posed is so enmeshed with political, institutional, and economic complexities that too much must not be expected from any program of research. Nevertheless, basic studies on relevant questions should help to distill some useful generalizations by which alternative economic policies may be judged, and it is in that spirit that the investigation is being launched.

The development of timely and comprehensive information on job vacancies throughout the United States may have a significant bearing on the problem just considered, both in promoting fuller employment directly and in providing guidance for fiscal and monetary policy. With the support of the Office of Manpower, Automation and Training of the U.S. Department of Labor, plans for a conference on the Measurement and Interpretation of Job Vacancies were pressed during 1964 and the conference was held in February 1965. Robert Ferber (University of Illinois) was chairman of the planning committee. The conference drew heavily upon experience abroad and obtained encouraging firsthand reports on experimental studies under way in this country. Further details about the conference will be found in Part V.

Policies aimed at simultaneous achievement of the goals of full employment, rapid growth in productivity, and a stable price level must reckon with the constraints imposed by the balance of payments—a fact of life that has become increasingly plain to American citizens in recent years. In other countries, the process of adjusting or correcting balance-of-payments deficits and surpluses has also received much attention. With a view to learning from our experience and that of other countries, an empirical study of adjustment processes and policies has been planned, and Michael Michaely (Hebrew University) will begin work on this project at the National Bureau in the autumn.

An exploratory study of banking markets and bank structure, designed to determine whether new studies in this field might be desirable and feasible, was begun. Donald P. Jacobs (Northwestern University) and George Morrison (Cornell University) are in charge of the exploration, aided by an advisory committee headed by Lester V. Chandler (Princeton University). A grant from the American Bankers Association is supporting the work. For a brief description of the study, see Part IV, section 4.

George Morrison was appointed a research fellow for 1964-65, under a grant provided by the Sloan Foundation. He is devoting his attention mainly to a study of cyclical changes in corporate stock and bond financing, and describes his plans in Part IV, section 4.

Studies of the quality of credit carried out at the National Bureau and elsewhere during recent years have resulted in a considerable expansion of statistical information on credit terms, the financial status of borrowers, and lending experience. But these materials are currently published in various sources and are relatively inaccessible. To help remedy this situation, Edgar Fiedler has agreed to undertake the preparation of a compendium that will present the data, describe their nature and sources, and contain a guide to their interpretation. This new work should admirably supplement the summary report on the credit quality studies that James Earley is preparing, and hopefully it may facilitate the wider use of these data in consideration of monetary and credit policies. The Bankers Trust Company is contributing substantially to the support of the study.

Consumer purchases of automobiles and household equipment have a vital bearing on the health and vigor of the economy. F. Thomas Juster's monograph, *Anticipations and Purchases: An Analysis of Consumer Behavior,* published last year, indicated that surveys of consumers' intentions to buy held some promise of aiding forecasts of actual purchases. Juster suggested that this promise might be improved by asking consumers to estimate the chances that they would buy an item, instead of merely asking whether they did or did not intend to do so. The Bureau of the Census has carried out an experimental survey to test this suggestion. Juster's analysis of the results, aided by a grant from the Automobile Manufacturers Association, Inc., should prove instructive. (See Part IV, section 2.)

STUDIES COMPLETED

Thirteen reports on research conducted by the staff have been published since January 1, 1964, and seven are in or about to go to press. The titles and authors of these reports are listed below, together with those of reports that will soon be ready for review by the Board. For a list of conference reports, see Part V.

REPORTS PUBLISHED SINCE
JANUARY 1, 1964

Anticipations and Purchases: An Analysis of Consumer Behavior, by F. Thomas Juster (General Series 79, 1964, xviii + 303 pp., $6.50). Investigates experience with surveys of consumer buying intentions and their fulfillment. Finds that intention surveys can make a significant contribution to the prediction of purchases of automobiles and other durable goods, and suggests ways to improve surveys to that end.

Consumer Sensitivity to Finance Rates: An Empirical and Analytical Investigation, by F. Thomas Juster and Robert P. Shay (Occasional Paper 88, 1964, xi + 105 pp., $2.50). Investigates the relation between finance rates charged on instalment credit contracts and the demand for credit, and develops a theoretical model for analysis of consumer borrowing decisions. Examines the extent of consumer knowledge of finance rates charged in instalment credit contracts, the relation between knowledge of rates and rate response, and how borrowing decisions may be influenced by the acquisition of finance rate knowledge.

Consumer Credit Costs, 1949-59, by Paul F. Smith (Studies in Consumer Instalment Financing 11, 1964, xix + 160 pp., $4.50). Explores the interrelations between rates of charge and major cost components of four principal types of financial institutions: consumer finance companies, sales finance companies, commercial banks, and federal credit unions. Analyzes the profitability of consumer credit operations during the ten-year period.

Human Capital: A Theoretical and Empirical Analysis, with Special Reference to Education, by Gary S. Becker (General Series 80, 1964, xvi + 187 pp., $5.00). This study presents estimates of rates of return on investment in human capital, mainly in the form of education. The author finds that not only does the individual benefit substantially but the return to society, in the form of higher productivity, is also greater. The study includes comparisons of the returns on high-school and college education to whites and nonwhites, males and females, urban and rural persons.

Evidences of Long Swings in Aggregate Construction Since the Civil War, by Moses Abramovitz (Occasional Paper 90, 1964, xii + 240 pp., $4.00). Part of a recurrent effort by the National Bureau to contribute to the knowledge of long swings in economic development, this study reviews and assesses the evidence bearing on the existence of these waves in aggregate construction and in the major types of construction in the United States.

Estimates of Residential Building, United States, 1840-1939, by Manuel Gottlieb (Technical

Paper 17, 1964, xvi + 99 pp., $2.00). Broadens the span of knowledge of American residential building by combining new information with older data. New estimates are provided for 1840-90 and, in addition, the study revises in an upward direction the presently accepted estimates for the years 1890-1939.

Research in the Capital Markets, National Bureau Exploratory Committee on Research in the Capital Markets (1964, v + 43 pp., $1.00). This report is the result of two meetings and extensive discussions of the National Bureau Exploratory Committee on Research in the Capital Markets. It contains an inventory of recent and current research and recommendations for further research, both in the capital markets as a whole and in particular sectors. It is a supplement to the May 1964 *Journal of Finance.*

The Flow of Capital Funds in the Postwar Economy, by Raymond W. Goldsmith (Studies in Capital Formation and Financing 12, 1965, xxi + 317 pp., $10.00). As the concluding volume in the National Bureau's Postwar Capital Market Study, this report presents the main features of the American capital market in the postwar period. It studies the fund flows for the main sectors of the economy and through five capital market instruments: U.S. Treasury securities, state and local government securities, corporate bonds, corporate stocks, and residential mortgages.

The Measurement of Corporate Sources and Uses of Funds, by David Meiselman and Eli Shapiro (Technical Paper 18, 1964, xvi + 281 pp., $4.50). Provides basic data on the flow of funds through the corporate business sector by major industry groupings. Covers all non-financial corporations reporting for tax purposes to the Internal Revenue Service, classified in the following industries: manufacturing, mining, gas and electric utilities, railroads, and communications; and trade, service, credit agencies other than banks, and miscellaneous corporations.

The Cyclical Behavior of the Term Structure of Interest Rates, by Reuben A. Kessel (Occasional Paper 91, 1965, viii + 113 pp., $3.00). The term structure of interest rates is analyzed chiefly according to the results of testing a modified version of the expectations hypothesis. The author explores whether such a modified hypothesis is consistent with the observed facts and, if so, whether the risk premium of long-term securities is positive or negative. He also makes use of an alternate interpretation of admitting risk premiums to the expectations hypothesis.

The Quality of Trade Credit, by Martin H. Seiden (Occasional Paper 87, 1964, xx + 129 pp., $3.00). A pioneering measurement of the volume, terms, and loss experience on trade credit for economic sectors and by size of creditor and debtor firm. Develops methods of analyzing risks attached to the extension of trade credit.

Productivity Trends in the Goods and Service Sectors, 1929-61: A Preliminary Survey, by Victor R. Fuchs (Occasional Paper 89, 1964, ix + 48 pp., $1.75). Presents new data on trends in productivity in the service sector and in other industries. The study points out some reasons why the growth of output per man in the service industries has lagged greatly behind that in other industries. It also indicates the areas most in need of further research in order to increase understanding of productivity change. The role of the quality of labor in productivity change is given special attention.

Business and Professional Income Under the Personal Income Tax, by C. Harry Kahn (Fiscal Studies 8, 1964, xx + 188 pp., $4.00). Deals with the tax treatment of individuals' income from sole proprietorships and partnerships in manufacturing, finance, trade, agriculture, and professional practice. Attention is paid to the changing relation, over time and cross-sectionally by size of income, between the sole proprietorship and partnership income and the total income of owners. The extent to which losses from business and professions are reported on tax returns with positive or negative total income is examined in detail, and its significance interpreted.

REPORTS IN PRESS

Determinants and Effects of Changes in the Stock of Money, 1875-1960, by Phillip Cagan (Studies in Business Cycles 13).

Costs, Prices, and Profits: Their Cyclical Relations, by Thor Hultgren (Studies in Business Cycles 14).

Trade Union Membership, 1897-1962, by Leo Troy (Occasional Paper 92).

Financial Adjustments to Unemployment, by Philip Klein (Occasional Paper 93).

REPORTS SOON TO GO TO PRESS

"Consumer Credit Finance Charges: Rate Information and Quotation," by Wallace P. Mors (Studies in Consumer Instalment Financing 12).

"Measuring Transactions Between World Areas," by Herbert Woolley (Studies in International Economic Relations 3).

"International Price Competitiveness: A Preliminary Report," by Irving B. Kravis, Robert E. Lipsey, and Philip J. Bourque (Occasional Paper 94).

REPORTS SOON TO BE SUBMITTED FOR APPROVAL

"Economic Aspects of Pensions," by Roger F. Murray (General Series).

"The Effect of Pension Plans on Aggregate Saving: Evidence from a Sample Survey," by Phillip Cagan (Occasional Paper).

"The Personal Exemptions in the Federal Income Tax," by Lawrence H. Seltzer (Fiscal Studies).

"The Treatment of Income from Employment Under the Individual Income Tax," by C. Harry Kahn (Fiscal Studies).

"The Behavior of Interest Rates: A Progress Report," by Joseph W. Conard (Occasional Paper).

"Changes in the Cyclical Behavior of Interest Rates," by Phillip Cagan (Occasional Paper).

"Orders and Production in Manufacturing Industries: A Cyclical Analysis," by Victor Zarnowitz (Studies in Business Cycles).

PUBLISHING ARRANGEMENTS

Effective September 1, 1964, Columbia University Press became the distributor of the National Bureau's books published prior to 1953 and since September 1, 1964, and of all Occasional Papers and Technical Papers.

Princeton University Press is the publisher and distributor of the books published by it for the National Bureau between 1953 and September 1, 1964.

PART IV

Staff Reports on Research Under Way

1. ECONOMIC GROWTH

TAX POLICIES FOR
ECONOMIC GROWTH

Our studies of the relation of taxation to the processes of economic growth have pursued two major lines of inquiry. We have directed part of our research, with the support of a grant from the Rockefeller Brothers Fund, to improving our knowledge of the effects of various features of business income taxation on the capacity and incentives of business enterprises to innovate and grow. We are also investigating the impact of the individual income tax on personal effort, saving, and investment, and on the willingness and financial capability of individuals to undertake business ventures. Support for this group of investigations comes from a grant from the Life Insurance Association of America.

The business income tax studies include the investigation by Challis A. Hall, Jr. (Yale University), of the effects of the federal corporation income tax on business policies affecting the pace and nature of corporation growth, on total private saving, and on the labor and capital shares of income originating in manufacturing corporations in the short run. A study by Thomas M. Stanback, Jr. (New York University), deals with the investment response of companies in the textile manufacturing industry to changes in 1954 and in 1961-62 in the tax rules governing depreciation. My survey of the use of alternative depreciation methods since 1954 also falls in this group.

In the individual income tax area, Roger F. Miller (University of Wisconsin) has under way an econometric analysis of capital gains taxation in relation to patterns of individual saving and investing. Daniel M. Holland (Massachusetts Institute of Technology) is measuring the extent of effective progression in tax liabilities of top corporate executives and, in an interview study, is attempting to assess the impact of graduation in marginal tax rates on the amount and character of effort by high-bracket individuals. C. Harry Kahn (Rutgers University) is analyzing the operation of the loss carry-over provisions in the case of unincorporated businesses and the effectiveness of alternative averaging systems in offsetting the bias against risk assumption inherent in a graduated income tax.

At midyear the report of the joint National Bureau–Brookings Institution conference, *The Role of Direct and Indirect Taxes in the Federal Revenue System,* was published. The report includes the papers prepared for the conference by John F. Due, Arnold C. Harberger, Richard Musgrave and Peggy Brewer Richman, Douglas Eldridge, and Otto Eckstein (assisted by Vito Tanzi); the formal discussions by E. Cary Brown, William Fellner, Harvey Brazer, Ronald Welch, Carl Shoup, Lawrence Krause, Fritz Neumark, and Dan T. Smith; and a summary of the conference discussion prepared by Samuel B. Chase, Jr.

Forthcoming in 1965 will be the report on a second joint conference of the National Bureau and the Brookings Institution, *Foreign Tax Policies and Economic Growth*. This volume will include papers by Francesco Forte, Cornelis Goedhart, Karl Hauser, Ryutaro Komiya, Leif Mutén and Karl O. Faxén, Pierre Tabatoni, and Alan Williams; discussions by Paul Senf, Fritz Neumark, Siro Lombardini, Lars Nabseth, Claes Sandels, J. Van Hoorn, Jr., A. J. van den Tempel, Sumio Hara, Makoto Yasui, Alan R. Prest, Robert Liebaut, D. de la Martinière; and a summary of the conference proceedings by E. Gordon Keith.

SURVEY OF THE USE OF ALTERNATIVE DEPRECIATION METHODS UNDER THE INTERNAL REVENUE CODE OF 1954

This survey examines the extent to which business income taxpayers have adopted the accelerated depreciation methods (declining balance or sum of years-digits) provided in the Internal Revenue Code of 1954. It is clear that the effects of such provisions on investment in depreciable facilities depend on how fully they are used.

The most recent data available and covered by this survey are for the taxable year 1960. In that year, about 24 per cent of corporate returns indicated use of the declining-balance method, compared with 14.6 per cent in 1957 and 7.6 per cent in 1954. On the other hand, the proportion of returns showing use of the sum of the years-digits method changed only slightly. It rose from 4.8 per cent in 1954 to 6.6 per cent in 1957, then fell to 5.9 in 1960. The rough estimate of the proportion of corporations using only the straight-line method fell from about 86 per cent in 1954 to 78 per cent in 1957 and 70 per cent in 1960. The proportionate amount of depreciation allowances computed under the accelerated methods also increased—from 26.6 per cent in 1957 to 39.2 per cent in 1960 (Table IV-1). As was the case for 1957, we also discovered in the 1960 corporation returns that the proportion of corporations using the accelerated methods increased with company size. So, too, did the amount of depreciation computed under accelerated methods (Table IV-2).

The amount of depreciable property to which each depreciation method is applied is in some respects a surer indicator of the extent of use of the accelerated methods than either the number of businesses showing use of these methods or the amount of depreciation generated thereby. In 1959, about 71.5 per cent of all corporate depreciable facilities then on hand were in straight-line accounts, 15.6 per cent were under declining-balance depreciation, and 10.3 per cent were in sum of the years-digits accounts (Table IV-3). The corresponding proportions for partnerships in 1959 were 63.5 per cent, 16.2 per cent, and 2.2 per cent. Corporate assets can be divided very roughly between those acquired before and those acquired after the end of 1953. Since only the latter are eligible for the accelerated methods, the respective proportions for these assets are a more useful indication of corporation response to the availability of the

TABLE IV-1

NUMBER OF CORPORATIONS AND AMOUNT OF DEPRECIATION BY
DEPRECIATION METHODS, 1957 AND 1960

	1957		1960	
Method of Depreciation	Number of Corporations	Amount of Depreciation (millions of dollars)	Number of Corporations	Amount of Depreciation (millions of dollars)
Straight line	720,693	11,888	769,515	11,223
Declining balance	108,646	2,630	194,913	4,673
Sum of years-digits	49,084	1,870	47,810	2,859
Other methods	4,410	537	4,485	473
Total	743,863	16,926	816,417	19,228
	(percentage distribution)			
Straight line	96.9	70.2	94.3	58.4
Declining balance	14.6	15.5	23.9	24.3
Sum of years-digits	6.6	11.1	5.9	14.9
Other methods	0.6	3.2	0.5	2.5
Straight line only[a]	78.2	—	69.7	—

SOURCE: For 1957, U.S. Treasury Department, Internal Revenue Service, special tabulation. For 1960, Joint Economic Committee, *Federal Tax System, Facts and Problems*, 1964, p. 256.

[a] The total number of corporations is less than the sum of the individual entries, since any one corporation may use different methods of depreciation for different assets. Only one method, however, can be used for any particular asset, so that the details do add to the totals shown in the columns on amount of depreciation.

Because of duplication noted between entries giving number of corporations, the percentage figures for those using only the straight-line method are minimum estimates obtained by subtracting the percentages for other methods from 100.

accelerated depreciation provisions. Of such facilities, only 45 per cent was in straight-line accounts and all but 1.5 per cent of the remainder was under accelerated methods. It seems likely that similarly larger proportions of the post-1953 facilities of partnerships were under the accelerated methods.

Among partnerships a pronounced tendency is evident for the proportionate amount of the property under the accelerated methods to increase with company size. Corporations show a similar tendency with respect to assets acquired after 1953. To a large extent, this reflects the proportionately greater use of the sum of the years-digits method by large than by small corporations. Thus, corporations with total assets of $25 million and over held 25.2 per cent of their post-1953 assets in sum of the years-digits accounts, while the corresponding figure is only 5.6 per cent for corporations with total assets of less than $1 million. The proportions relating to the use of the declining-balance method by the two groups on post-1953 assets are not so far apart.

Substantial differences in the proportionate amounts of property under the accelerated methods are also found among industries. In the partnership group, companies in the finance, insurance, and real estate division—which incidentally held larger amounts of depreciable facilities than any other division in 1959—had the largest proportion of such facilities in accelerated-method accounts, fol-

TABLE IV-2

PERCENTAGE DISTRIBUTION OF CORPORATIONS AND OF AMOUNT OF DEPRECIATION BY METHOD OF DEPRECIATION AND BY SIZE OF TOTAL ASSETS, 1960

Size of Total Assets	Straight Line	Declining Balance	Sum of Years-Digits	Other	Straight Line Only[a]
		NUMBER OF CORPORATIONS			
Under $100,000	94.6	16.6	2.8	0.3	80.3
100,000 to under 500,000	93.6	30.9	7.8	0.6	60.8
500,000 to under 1,000,000	94.0	38.6	12.3	0.8	48.4
1,000,000 to under 5,000,000	94.3	40.7	16.2	1.6	41.5
5,000,000 to under 10,000,000	96.9	37.8	19.3	2.3	40.6
10,000,000 to under 50,000,000	97.5	37.5	21.0	3.5	38.1
50,000,000 to under 100,000,000	98.0	40.9	28.9	6.7	23.5
100,000,000 and over	97.2	46.7	34.8	11.0	7.6
Total	94.3	23.9	5.9	0.6	69.7
		AMOUNT OF DEPRECIATION[b]			
Under $100,000	79.7	16.2	2.6	0.4	—
100,000 to under 500,000	67.7	25.7	5.0	0.5	—
500,000 to under 1,000,000	63.0	29.1	6.5	0.6	—
1,000,000 to under 5,000,000	58.6	29.6	9.5	1.8	—
5,000,000 to under 10,000,000	57.3	25.9	13.9	2.7	—
10,000,000 to under 50,000,000	56.9	25.6	14.9	2.5	—
50,000,000 to under 100,000,000	52.2	26.2	18.3	3.3	—
100,000,000 and over	52.9	22.6	21.0	3.5	—
Total	58.2	24.2	14.8	2.5	—

SOURCE: See Table IV-1.
[a] See footnote a, Table IV-1.
[b] Detail will not add to 100 per cent because of the exclusion of small amounts of so-called additional first-year depreciations.

lowed by construction and mining, with manufacturing partnerships ranking sixth in the nine divisions. Among corporations, on the other hand, manufacturing companies held over two-thirds of their post-1953 facilities in accelerated-method accounts (Table IV-4). Public utilities actually held a slightly larger proportion of such facilities in declining-balance accounts, but a smaller proportion under sum of the years-digits method, than did manufacturing corporations.

The alternative measures—number of companies, amount of depreciation, and amount of assets—employed in examining the use of accelerated depreciation methods result in differing conclusions about the extent to which these methods have been adopted. In terms of both the amount of depreciation and the amount of property, the shift from straight-line to the accelerated methods has been extensive. From the point of view of number of companies, one must conclude that use of these methods, though increasing, remains narrowly confined.

TABLE IV-3

Cost of Depreciable Assets of Corporations by Method of Depreciation and by Size of Total Assets, All Assets on Hand in 1959 and Assets Acquired After 1953 and on Hand in 1959

Size of Total Assets	Straight Line	Declining Balance	Sum of Years-Digits	Other Methods	Total
		A. ALL ASSETS ON HAND IN 1959 (thousands of dollars)			
Under $1,000,000	14,489,931	4,008,979	751,795	14,575	19,265,280
1,000,000 under 25,000,000	4,894,480	2,047,776	399,134	15,363	7,356,753
25,000,000 and over	135,646,467	27,811,915	21,078,505	5,767,294	190,304,181
Total	155,030,878	33,868,670	22,229,434	5,797,232	216,926,214
		(percentage distribution)			
Under $1,000,000	75.2	20.8	3.9	0.1	100.0
1,000,000 under 25,000,000	66.5	27.8	5.4	0.2	100.0
25,000,000 and over	71.3	14.6	11.1	3.0	100.0
Total	71.5	15.6	10.3	2.7	100.0
		B. ASSETS ACQUIRED AFTER 1953 AND ON HAND IN 1959 (thousands of dollars)			
Under $1,000,000	9,007,570	3,627,003	743,276	14,244	13,392,093
1,000,000 under 25,000,000	2,642,074	1,740,006	393,228	7,466	4,782,774
25,000,000 and over	34,006,310	26,875,843	20,979,641	1,526,414	83,388,208
Total	45,655,954	32,242,852	22,116,145	1,548,124	101,563,075
		(percentage distribution)			
Under $1,000,000	67.3	27.1	5.6	0.1	100.0
1,000,000 under 25,000,000	55.2	36.4	8.2	0.2	100.0
25,000,000 and over	40.8	32.2	25.2	1.8	100.0
Total	45.0	31.8	21.8	1.5	100.0

Source: Internal Revenue Service, *Life of Depreciable Assets Source Book*.
Note: Detail will not add to totals because of rounding.

The data suggest a positive association between company size and both the proportion of companies using the accelerated methods and the proportion of assets in accelerated-method accounts. Use of the accelerated methods does not appear to be systematically associated with industrial division, type of asset, or service life of the facilities. No obvious explanation for this association between company size and use of accelerated depreciation methods is suggested by the data. None of the constraints imposed by statute and regulation on the use of these methods can be reasonably construed as exerting a bias against their adoption by small companies. Whatever the explanation, the fact revealed by these data is that the advantages of accelerated depreciation have accrued primarily to

TABLE IV-4

Cost of Depreciable Assets of Corporations Acquired After 1953 and on Hand in 1959, by Method of Depreciation and by Industrial Division

		Method of Depreciation			
Industrial Division	Total	Straight Line	Declining Balance	Sum of Years-Digits	Other Methods
	(millions of dollars)				
Agriculture	363	301	57	6	a
Mining	2,091	1,387	434	52	218
Construction	944	590	301	53	a
Manufacturing	41,394	13,215	13,557	14,178	444
Public utilities	38,624	19,116	12,788	5,874	846
Trade	4,948	3,095	884	940	29
Finance, insurance, real estate	10,359	6,279	3,322	749	9
Services	2,814	1,652	899	262	1
Not allocable	25	23	2	a	a
Total	101,563	45,656	32,243	22,116	1,548
	(percentage distribution)				
Agriculture	100.0	82.8	15.6	1.5	0.1
Mining	100.0	66.3	20.8	2.5	10.4
Construction	100.0	62.4	31.9	5.6	a
Manufacturing	100.0	31.9	32.8	34.3	1.1
Public utilities	100.0	49.5	33.1	15.2	2.2
Trade	100.0	62.6	17.9	19.0	0.6
Finance, insurance, real estate	100.0	60.6	32.1	7.2	0.1
Services	100.0	58.7	31.9	9.3	a
Not allocable	100.0	90.8	7.8	1.1	0.4
Total	100.0	45.0	31.8	21.8	1.5

SOURCE: Internal Revenue Service, *Life of Depreciable Assets Source Book*.
NOTE: Detail will not add to totals because of rounding.
[a] Less than $500,000 or less than .05 per cent.

a relatively small number of large companies. Our estimate is that corporations with total assets of $25 million or more account for all but an insignificant part of the roughly $2.5 billion difference between actual corporate depreciation allowances in 1959 and the amount that would have been claimed had only the straight-line method been available.

NORMAN B. TURE

CORPORATE PROFITS TAXATION AND ECONOMIC GROWTH

My efforts during the past year have been directed toward summarizing the results of interviews with executives on the effects of the corporation income tax on company growth. The growth-oriented activities include capital expenditures, introduction of new products and processes, and research and development activities.

During the interview phase of the project, I collected a great deal of material on corporate growth activities, including company reports, sections from capital expenditure manuals outlining methods of calculating the rate of return on new investment, and other aspects of capital budgeting. The interviews alone have provided very extensive information.

This material must be condensed and organized by categories before company practices and attitudes can meaningfully be delineated and compared. During the year I was also able to compile from annual reports descriptive statistical material on almost all fifty companies in the sample. For some forty-five of these companies, I examined and summarized the rate-of-return formulas and the responses to interview questions on this subject.

This work of summarization and organization will be completed shortly. It will then be possible to start tabulating the replies to questions for the whole sample of companies.

CHALLIS A. HALL, JR.

EFFECT OF CHANGES IN TAX LAWS
ON MODERNIZATION EXPENDITURES
IN THE TEXTILE INDUSTRY

There are two principal avenues by which acceleration of depreciation for tax purposes may influence modernization expenditures. (1) It may serve to increase the demand for modern equipment and plant. (2) It may increase the supply of funds which the firm finds it justifiable to spend for such purposes. Both routes depend upon tax savings which occur in the earlier years of life of the new asset as a result of acceleration. The increase in demand may occur as a result of an increase in the expected rate of return, a reduction of the after-tax payback period, a reduction in optimum service life and shortening of replacement cycle, and a reduction of the period in which funds are at risk. An increase in the supply of available funds is important if the firm has an aversion to use of long-term debt or deems the cost of such funds significantly higher than the opportunity cost of using internally generated funds.

In practice, some of the effects indicated may come through a change in management attitudes and objectives relating to modernization expenditures. Management acts in a world of uncertainty and under conditions in which there are competing demands for funds. Frequently the budget for modernization expenditures is not determined by rate-of-return calculations; when this is the case, the amount of depreciation charged is likely to provide an important basis for its determination. If the firm accepts tax depreciation as the basis for its regular (book) depreciation charges, an acceleration of depreciation will affect the modernization budget. As another example, management may tend to look at the amount of undepreciated book value when deciding whether or not an asset should be replaced. Accelerated depreciation practices, if they alter book depreciation, serve to reduce undepreciated book value of plant and equipment more rapidly, thereby diminishing this deterrent to replacement.

This study is an investigation of such possible effects of recent changes in depreciation provisions and of the introduction of the investment tax credit on modernization in the textile industry. The industry was selected for examination because the provision for shorter service lives for tax depreciation purposes was made by the authorities a year earlier than in other industries, and because a relatively large proportion of the industry's equipment was widely thought to be in need of replacement at the time of the change.

The investigation has been conducted principally by interviewing executives of twenty-five textile firms and five leading textile machinery manufacturers. In addition, data relating to borrowing, cash flow, and capital expenditures of the reporting firms and of certain other textile firms are being analyzed in order to verify or supplement, where possible, the evidence obtained from the interviews.

The objective of the study is to determine the extent to which accelerated depreciation, or the investment credit, has influenced modernization expenditure decisions via any of the routes mentioned above. In general, evidence points to the following:

1. Only a minority of firms use after-tax computation of rate of return on investment, discounted cash flow, or payback which would permit an explicit recognition of the increased after-tax returns available as a result of such tax revisions.

2. On the other hand, all firms recognize that provisions for accelerated depreciation increase internal cash flow. A large majority are averse to any long-term borrowing or borrow only occasionally for major expansion in capacity or ventures into new product lines. Although a few firms appear to have been virtually unaffected in their expenditures by increased cash flow, a much larger number seem to have been significantly influenced. Some of these firms testify to having labored under continuing cash limitations. Others appear to carry out the decision-making process under conditions in which cash constraints are only one of a number of constraints, which include managerial limitations and uncertainties as to market possibilities and anticipated rate of technological obsolescence. Cash flow from depreciation is therefore only one of several variables and its exact effect is difficult to pin down. Both the interviews and the statistical evidence, however, point to a positive relation with investment decisions.

3. There is considerable evidence that accelerated depreciation alters managerial attitudes and objectives. In most of the firms, "book" depreciation is made to conform to tax depreciation. Depreciation charges in many instances provide at least an informal basis for preliminary allocation of funds to modernization expenditures. Moreover, in a number of cases executives and directors are influenced in their willingness to replace equipment by the amount of undepreciated value that remains on the company's books.

A draft is in preparation, and it is expected that a manuscript will be ready for a reading committee within the next two months.

THOMAS M. STANBACK, JR.

PERSONAL CAPITAL GAINS TAXATION AND ECONOMIC GROWTH

This is an econometric investigation of the nature and magnitude of the impact of the present tax treatment of capital gains and losses on individuals' decisions with respect to the total volume of their personal savings, transferring accumulated savings among alternative earning assets, the riskiness of their portfolios, and the manner in which their current savings are translated into real investment. The study uses detailed panel data on incomes and their major components, including dividends and realized capital gains, obtained from a sample of Wisconsin individual income tax returns, 1947-59, supplemented by data on some of the same individuals from other sources.

During the past year we have gone a long way toward completing the acquisition of the data and processing them into usable form. The names of the companies paying dividends and interest to each taxpayer, and the amounts each taxpayer received from each company, have been coded, punched, and put on tape in order to allow capitalization of the receipts and determine the number and value of securities held. Supplementary data on age, race, covered incomes, and covered quarters have been obtained for most of the sample from the Social Security Administration.

A major accomplishment was the interview survey carried out last spring and summer.

The survey provided some detailed asset and income information not shown on returns as well as replies to some motivational questions. Reasonably complete responses were received from a stratified sample of approximately 1,100 persons. These responses have been coded and edited, and the keypunching is well along.

Our current efforts are largely devoted to the integration of the data derived from different sources into single consistent records for each individual. Some frustrating delays in programming have been experienced, but are being slowly overcome.

ROGER F. MILLER

THE TAX TREATMENT OF
FLUCTUATING INCOMES

During the past year work has gone forward on writing a program to test the efficacy of various types of provisions designed to mitigate the effect of fluctuating incomes on income tax liability. At least initially, my empirical research effort is concentrated in the area of the individual income tax, where a bias against fluctuating incomes is most evident in view of the imposition of tax at graduated rates. In the corporate sector the problem may be less acute, since for the most part the corporate tax has no graduation. The program referred to is to test current loss carry-over and averaging provisions on a sample of returns for identical Wisconsin taxpayers filed during the period 1947-59. A tape containing a preliminary sample of Wisconsin taxpayers was obtained during the year to test the program, but difficulties with it caused some unforeseen delays. A new tape is expected soon.

In the meantime I have turned my efforts to writing an exposition of the several conceptual problems relative to loss carry-overs and averaging that require clarification and discussion at the outset. It is hoped that this exposition will furnish a draft for the first chapter of the final monograph summarizing this study.

C. HARRY KAHN

EFFECT OF TAXATION ON PERSONAL EFFORT

Our study of the effect of taxation on executives' effort follows three main lines of investigation:

1. Wilbur G. Lewellen has assumed primary responsibility for the investigation of what top executives—the four or five most highly paid officers in the biggest companies—have received as additional nonsalary compensation over the last twenty-five years. To this end, a method of placing the major nonsalary components of compensation—pensions, other deferred compensation, and stock options—on a basis comparable with salary has been developed. A program for deriving these salary equivalents has been written, and data for over 500 executives in 50 companies have been assembled and edited and are ready for processing. There are between 200 and 250 executives for whom we shall have, for every year from 1939 through 1962, an estimate of total after-tax compensation, as well as the proportions accounted for by salary, bonus, prospective pension benefits, stock options, and other deferred compensation arrangements. In addition to this information, other points can be illuminated by these time series. For example, knowing each executive's age, we will be able to ascertain the changes in the span of working life and in retirement age. A first draft should be finished by the end of June, and a full version by the end of September.

2. The second approach concerns a broader sample of executives. The data are cross-sectional and permit us to calculate effective rates of tax of persons who can be identified roughly from tax returns as business executives. For both 1960 and 1962, samples of about 100,000 personal income tax returns

are available. To designate all persons with wages and salaries of over, say, $25,000 as executives is, of course, arbitrary, but it probably comes fairly close to the mark. For this group of returns we can calculate, for example, the effective rates of tax, the importance of capital gains and deductions in determining this result, and the dispersion of effective and marginal rates. A program for this purpose has been written, and the results will soon be ready for analysis.

3. The third line of inquiry comprises interviews with business executives designed to discover what influence taxes may have on such matters as the choice of a business career, decisions to accept or reject promotion and to remain with a firm or join another, the form in which compensation is arranged, and the effect which these questions, in turn, may have on other decisions and activities, including time devoted to both personal and business tax questions. The interviews have been my main concern over the year and will continue to be so through May or June. I expect to complete a first draft of a report on them over the summer and to have a first draft of a report on the whole project before the end of the year.

DANIEL M. HOLLAND

PRODUCTIVITY IN THE SERVICE INDUSTRIES

This study, undertaken with the aid of a Ford Foundation grant, is aimed at measuring and analyzing inputs, outputs, and productivity in the service sector. We are attempting to identify the factors responsible for productivity change as well as those that inhibit improvements in efficiency in this sector. Our work has been organized along three major lines. First, we have undertaken studies of individual industries. Second, we have planned studies of problems that cut across all or most of the service industries. Finally, I am attempting to view the sector as a whole and to contrast it with the rest of the economy.

The first publication resulting from the project was my *Productivity Trends in the Goods and Service Sectors, 1929-61: A Preliminary Survey* (Occasional Paper 89), which appeared in October 1964. I am presently revising a draft of a second paper, "The Growing Importance of the Service Sector." My contribution to Part II of this report draws on portions of this paper. A talk based on an earlier draft was given at the annual meeting of the American Statistical Association in Chicago in December 1964.

During the past year I began a study of productivity in health. We have been collecting data concerning inputs such as hospital facilities and employment; our principal attention, however, has been given to the problem of measuring the output of the health industry. This has customarily been measured by number of physician-visits and number of hospital patient-days, but it seems to me that output should be reflected in the *health* of the population.

One important, readily available, and objective measure of health is the death rate. I am investigating the relations over time and among states and countries between death rates and inputs of health resources, income, industrialization, and other economic and social variables. The problem is complicated because neither death rates nor any other index alone or in combination provides a completely acceptable measure of health. Moreover, there are many things that affect health other than the efforts of the health industry. Nevertheless, I anticipate that some useful insights into the economic aspects of health will emerge from this approach.

As is often true of research in relatively unexplored areas, our work in the service sector has raised a number of questions the importance of which was not obvious to us at the inception of the project. We find that we need to know more about the elasticity of substitution of skilled for unskilled labor, the income elasticity of demand for services, the role of the consumer in the production of services, the effects on productivity of self-employment and part-time employment, and the relation between productivity and transaction size. We expect to begin work on some of these questions in the near future.

Harry Gilman is studying changes in labor input in the service industries, with special attention to quality of labor and hours of work. Reports by other members of the project follow.

VICTOR R. FUCHS

PRODUCTIVITY GROWTH IN DISTRIBUTION

Progress is being made both in the measurement and analysis of changes in output, input, and productivity in retailing and wholesaling over the period 1929-58. One of the major elements in the increase in productivity in distribution, especially in the retailing of food, has been the increase in the average size of transaction. I present here the argument and the evidence concerning this increase.

The length of a production run is an important variable affecting productivity, as Armen Alchian suggested in a paper some years ago. Associated with each run is an element of fixed cost, e.g., setting up and closing a run and the delay between runs. Productivity therefore increases as the length of runs increases. Output changes usually consist of both changes in the length and in the number of runs; increases in output therefore usually raise productivity.

Both in retailing and in wholesaling, the "run" is a single transaction; costs of selling, billing, collecting, and delivering vary with the number as well as the dollar value of purchases. Several studies of checkout operations in food stores have established that the sales volume per man-hour, or labor productivity, as usually measured for any type of store, rises rapidly with the average size of transaction. Quantity discounts in wholesaling explicitly recognize the economies of transaction size.

The average size of transaction varies with the prices and the quantities of items purchased at any one time and, therefore, with the level of income. Gary Becker has maintained, moreover, that time has a price which increases with wages; time-consuming activities will decline as wages rise. Shopping for food is more frequent than shopping for other goods; therefore, assuming equal income elasticities of demand, the average size of purchases of food will rise more as income rises than the average size of purchases of other goods. Finally, the growth in the use of automobiles and the improvements in home storage facilities also contributed to the tendency toward larger purchases, particularly of food, which in large quantities becomes bulky.

The Super Market Institute reported that the average size of transaction in 1958 in supermarkets was $4.58. Even after correcting for the higher price level, this is much larger than the average purchase in food stores during the thirties, which amounted to about 50 cents. Supermarkets have been successful because they have facilitated large purchases, and they accomplished this by instituting self-service, by supplying a large assortment of goods, and by providing parking facilities. The appeal of the early supermarkets in the twenties and early thirties was based solely on price; during and after the forties their rapid growth was primarily a response to changes in consumers' shopping preferences.

The importance of transaction size in food retailing is demonstrated by a finding that sales per person engaged are directly related to family income and automobile usage. A regression analysis of sales per person engaged in food stores, as reported by the Census of Distribution for 188 Standard Metropolitan Statistical Areas in 1958, produced the following results:

$$p = 2.99 + .47i + .19g - .04d \quad (1)$$
$$ (.05) \quad (.04) \quad (.01)$$
$$R^2 = .50$$

All variables are expressed in logarithms, and
$p =$ sales per person engaged in food stores
$i =$ median family income
$g =$ gasoline sales per family
$d =$ population per square mile

The variables i and g are highly significant.

The objection may be made that average sales per store rise with sales and therefore with income; economies of scale are realized where incomes are high. If only the level of sales mattered, sales per family should have at least as large an effect as family income on sales per person engaged in food stores. When we substitute sales per family (f) for family income (i) in equation (1), we obtain the following results:

$$p = 4.71 + .16f + .31g - .001d \quad (2)$$
$$\quad\quad\quad (.06) \quad (.04) \quad (.009)$$
$$R^2 = .26$$

While f is highly significant, its effect on p is much smaller than that of i.

Among food stores, sales per person engaged vary with size of store as measured by sales. The relationship usually is attributed to the indivisibility of the small staff and the frequent lack of self-service in small stores. Another important element is the association between sales size and average value of transaction, because customers wishing to make a large purchase will seek a store where a large assortment is conveniently displayed. Small purchases are still made in small and more conveniently located groceries. That this is so can readily be determined by adding the variable, average sales size of food stores (s), to equation (1). The results are as follows:

$$p = 2.89 + .29i + .06g - .04d + .15s \quad (3)$$
$$\quad\quad\quad (.06) \quad (.04) \quad (.01) \quad (.03)$$
$$R^2 = .62$$

The interrelation of s with i reduces the regression coefficient associated with i, and similarly with g. Large food stores succeed where incomes and automobile usage are high, and their success reflects the effect of these variables on transaction size rather than economies of scale.

As incomes have risen, the variety of foods consumed, particularly of prepared foods, has increased. As a result, the proportion of total food purchases which are unplanned has risen; today more items are being selected by the purchaser while shopping than planned in advance. The display of a large variety of goods is a major attraction, and the competition of supermarkets, therefore, takes the form of increases in the number of items, which, in turn, reduce inventory turnover and increase space requirements. The staples of the trade have a high turnover, but represent a declining fraction of total business.

The survival of the corner grocery seems to be partly accounted for by this development. Those that survive are in a far stronger competitive position than the average small store of thirty years ago. Supermarkets are burdened by their slow-turnover merchandise, while the corner grocery caters to the demand for staples. This is one reason the small stores' operating expense ratios today are not much out of line with those of large stores.

The change in average transaction value in other types of store is being investigated. It does not appear to have been nearly as great as in food stores. Transaction values have risen in wholesaling with the increase in the average size of stores, and they probably explain a large part of the increase in productivity.

I am also investigating changes in the quality of labor. Increases in labor quality in retail trade have lagged behind those in other industries. The level of education of employees has not risen as rapidly, and the importance of teenage labor has increased more than elsewhere. The change in average weekly hours also is being measured. In addition, I shall estimate the change in the quantity of capital.

DAVID SCHWARTZMAN

STATE AND LOCAL GOVERNMENTS

The importance to the national economy of raising productivity in state and local government operations is considerable. Employment at this level now accounts for 77 per cent of all civilian government employment, 15 per cent of the total service sector, and 8 per cent of total U.S. employment. Moreover, it has been the most rapidly growing area of the economy in recent years, as may be seen in Table IV-5.

I find that there has been little substitution of capital for labor in state and local government operations; physical capital per worker is approximately the same as in 1929. This suggests that there may not have been much technological change either, because such change in other industries has usually been accompanied by an increase in capital per worker.

I am preparing a manuscript that will describe trends in employment and other inputs since 1929; report the result of interstate cross-section analysis for 1942, 1952, and 1962; and discuss inferences about productivity that are suggested by the trends and interstate differences.

ERNEST KURNOW

BARBER AND BEAUTY SHOPS

I am completing a manuscript on productivity and employment in barber and beauty shops. These two personal service industries have experienced quite different trends in output, employment, and productivity, as may be seen in Table IV-6. Much of my paper is concerned with exploring the reasons for this difference.

Barbering has been a relatively static industry in which the few important changes, such as the development of the safety razor, have had their major impact on output and productivity in the home rather than in the market. Beauty shops, on the other hand, have benefited from numerous technological advances (e.g., the cold wave, improved hair dyes), a sharply expanded demand (related to changes in technology, income, and fashion), and the growing use of part-time workers to minimize the waste of idle labor.

One interesting by-product of the study is the discovery that the observed high prices for haircuts do not result in high hourly earn-

TABLE IV-5

GROWTH OF EMPLOYMENT IN STATE AND LOCAL GOVERNMENT AND OTHER SECTORS OF THE ECONOMY, 1947-63

	Persons Engaged 1947	1963	Average Annual Rate of Change 1947-63
	(thousands)		(per cent)
State and local general government	3,053	5,841	4.1
Education	1,364	2,886	4.8
General government, excluding education	1,689	2,955	3.6
Federal civilian government	1,416	1,772	1.4
Total service sector	26,320	37,962	2.3
Total economy	57,652	69,411	1.2

SOURCE: U.S. Department of Commerce, Office of Business Economics.

ings for barbers. As Table IV-7 shows, barbers earn much less per hour than would be "expected" on the basis of their age, education, color, and sex. This is not true of beauticians. Part of the explanation seems to be that barbers suffer from large amounts of idle time.

JEAN WILBURN

LONG SWINGS IN THE GROWTH OF POPULATION AND LABOR FORCE

The purposes of this study, conceived within the framework of Abramovitz' inquiry into long swings in the economy as a whole, are, first, to describe long swings in the growth of population and labor force of the United States over the past century; second, to determine as far as possible the factors responsible for these swings; third, to see what light the long-swings approach can throw on the determinants of population and labor force growth in recent decades; and fourth, to consider the implications of the findings for projections to 1970 and later. Previous publications are *The American Baby Boom in Historical Perspective,* Occasional Paper 79, and "Influences in European Overseas Emigration before World War I," in *Economic Development and Cultural Change,* April 1961. Since July 1, 1963, the study has been supported by funds provided by the Office of Manpower, Automation and Training.

The plan of work in the past year has been to prepare three papers which distill the main conclusions of the study and provide the framework for a summary monograph. The first of these was presented last June to the Population Association of America, entitled "Long Swings in U.S. Demographic and Economic Growth: Some Findings on the Historical Pattern." The paper summarizes our findings on the nature of long swings in the growth of U.S. population and labor force, and on their apparent cause-effect relations in the period prior to World War I to similar movements in the rate of economic development. It will be published in Volume II of the Association's new journal, *Demography.*

TABLE IV-6

EMPLOYMENT, OUTPUT, AND PRODUCTIVITY IN BARBER AND BEAUTY SHOPS, 1939-58

	Barber Shops			*Beauty Shops*		
	1939	1958	Average Annual Rate of Change, 1939-58 (per cent)	1939	1958	Average Annual Rate of Change, 1939-58 (per cent)
Employment (thousands of full-time equivalents)	141	139	−.1	189	246	1.4
Receipts (current dollars in millions)	231	783	6.6	250	1,028	7.7
Receipts (constant 1948 dollars in millions)	439	486	.5	458	831	3.2
Prices (1948 = 100)	52.6	161.2	6.1	54.6	123.7	4.4
Real output per man (line 3 ÷ line 1)	3,110	3,490	.6	2,420	3,380	1.8

SOURCE: U.S. Bureau of Census, *Census of Business, Selected Services, 1939, 1958;* U.S. Bureau of Labor Statistics, *Consumer Price Index.*

TABLE IV-7

COMPARISON OF ACTUAL AND "EXPECTED" AVERAGE HOURLY EARNINGS OF BARBERS AND BEAUTICIANS, 1959

	Hourly Earnings		Actual ÷ Expected
	Actual	Expected	
Barbers	$1.69	$2.34	.72
Beauticians	1.62	1.79	.91

SOURCE: U.S. Bureau of the Census, *U.S. Census of Population and Housing: 1960, 1/1,000, 1/10,000.*

NOTE: Expected hourly earnings are based on classifying all workers into 144 groups according to age, education, color, and sex, and applying the "all industry" hourly earnings rate for each group to the number of barbers and beauticians in each group. "All industry" earnings rates calculated by Harry Gilman for the NBER service industry project.

A second paper, focusing on the period since World War I and considering implications for the future, is now in preparation. A third, "On Swings in Demographic and Economic Growth," provides an overview of the study and considers some of the more general aspects of the Kuznets-cycle concept. This paper, which will be presented at the United Nations World Population Conference in Belgrade in September 1965, has been completed and submitted to the U.N. In addition, a preliminary memorandum on the methodological aspects of the framework used in analyzing manpower change has been prepared. This will ultimately form part of the appendixes of the summary monograph. A draft of the monograph itself is planned for June 1965.

RICHARD A. EASTERLIN

LONG SWINGS IN URBAN BUILDING ACTIVITY

My manuscript on long swings in urban building was reviewed by a staff committee, in the course of which the scope of the work, its internal layout, and the analysis at critical points were considered. The upshot was a decision to confine the forthcoming monograph to a treatment of long swings in urban building and associated developments in realty markets and demographic activity, but to defer work, for the time being, on national swings. I have since reworked the manuscript to exclude, where applicable, the treatment of national swings and to order the flow of analysis of local long swings in some thirty urban areas.

The new order of presentation results in six chapters in the following sequence:

1. Introduction and Summary
2. Procedures, Sources, and Techniques
3. Long Cycles in Building Activity
4. Long Cycles in Real Estate Market Activity
5. Migration, Marriage, and Vacancy
6. Value and Price Adaptations

Chapters 3 and 4 deal with what happens in the realm of new building both as a whole and by types, and with accompanying shifts in real estate purchases, mortgage lending, lot development, and foreclosure. Chapters 5 and 6 trace the processes of long swings in a way that sheds light on the causal forces at work. In Chapter 5 these causal forces are related to the surging tides of demographic growth and the alternating waves of over- and under-building reflected in the systematic behavior of vacancies. In Chapter 6 these causal forces are related to the differential response of price and value levels and their crucial margins, which in turn reflect and grow out of varied patterns of market behavior and price formation and varied elasticities of supply.

In addition to revision of the manuscript, which is now being retyped, I have during the year prepared two papers related to the research project. One of these will be included in the forthcoming volume of the Conference on Research in Income and Wealth as a study of "Ohio Building, 1837-1912." A second paper, "New Measures of Value of Nonfarm Building U.S.A. Annually, 1850-1939," to be published in the *Review of Economics and Statistics,* amplifies my earlier Technical Paper 17 and its estimates of a new nationwide series of nonfarm residential unit construction between 1840-1939 by providing new estimates for the value of total nonfarm building for most of the same years.

MANUEL GOTTLIEB

ECONOMIC GROWTH OF THE SOVIET UNION

The object of this study, begun in 1954 under a grant from the Rockefeller Foundation, is to set forth and analyze the evidence bearing on the rate of economic growth of the Soviet economy. The work was undertaken in full recognition of the inherent difficulty of arriving at an answer and of the special problems in securing reliable information.

To date, publications resulting from the study include the following: *Some Observations on Soviet Industrial Growth,* by G. Warren Nutter (Occasional Paper 55, New York, NBER, 1957); *Freight Transportation in the Soviet Union: A Comparison with the United States,* by Ernest W. Williams, Jr. (Occasional Paper 65, New York, NBER, 1959); *Soviet Statistics of Physical Output of Industrial Commodities: Their Compilation and Quality,* by Gregory Grossman (Princeton University Press for NBER, 1960); *Small-Scale Industry in the Soviet Union,* by Adam Kaufman (Occasional Paper 80, New York, NBER, 1962); *Growth of Industrial Production in the Soviet Union,* by G. Warren Nutter (Princeton University Press for NBER, 1962); *Freight Transportation in the Soviet Union, Including Comparisons with the United States,* by Ernest W. Williams, Jr. (Princeton University Press for NBER, 1962). In addition, a *Statistical Abstract of Industrial Output in the Soviet Union, 1913-1955* (Parts 1-5, offset, 1957) was made available to scholars working on Soviet statistics.

Work continues on the agricultural sector, on industrial production, and on a summary volume.

With regard to agriculture, present plans include several papers—one on output, another on income, and a third on labor input. Under the direction of D. Gale Johnson, Arcadius Kahan is devoting his attention to output and income, and Douglas Diamond to labor. A more detailed statement on the work on Soviet agricultural labor is given below.

Indexes of industrial production originally published in *Growth of Industrial Production in the Soviet Union* have been revised and brought up to date in accord with information released in the last few years. An Occasional Paper discussing these revisions is being prepared.

The summary volume will combine the major findings for individual sectors and discuss such other matters as population, employment, construction, and standard of living. Work on the summary volume has been delayed by continuing difficulties in completing the study of the agricultural sector, largely because of problems raised by gaps and changes in the Soviet statistics of agriculture. It is hoped, however, that a preliminary report, now being written in the form of an Occasional Paper, will soon be available, and that it will be followed by the summary volume itself, as soon as the agricultural monographs are completed.

G. WARREN NUTTER

USE OF LABOR IN SOVIET AGRICULTURE

The objective of the study is to develop measures of employment in Soviet agriculture extending from the precollectivization period, 1925-29, to the early 1960's. To this end alternative series of the labor force in agriculture have been derived, differing in concept of employment. In addition, a series of workdays expended in agricultural production activity has been obtained.

The labor force principally or only occupied in farming was reduced by one-half between 1928 and 1962 (present-day boundaries). On the other hand, the measure of the input of labor expressed as workdays shows only a small decline—less than 5 per cent—between the two years. The strong divergency in trend between the size of the labor force and the measure of work done is primarily due to two phenomena: (1) an increase in the number of days per year worked by the average person in the farm labor force, and (2) a great expansion of the number of persons with a secondary employment in agriculture. The latter group, *principally* employed in nonfarm activity, is estimated at 36 million in 1958, a number equivalent to three-fourths of the 47 million principally or only occupied in farm work. Thus some 83 million persons, or more than one of every two persons in the population age 12 and over, participated at some time during the year in farm work.

Most of the labor force secondarily employed in agriculture reside in urban or suburban areas, and farming activity for this group is mostly limited to private holdings of a kitchen garden and livestock. This type of private subsidiary economy has been permitted to rapidly expand since the precollectivization period and provides an important supplement to the country's food production.

Both the summary paper and main body of the report will be concluded in 1965.

DOUGLAS B. DIAMOND

OTHER STUDIES

The following reports concerned with economic growth were published: *Evidences of Long Swings in Aggregate Construction Since the Civil War,* by Moses Abramovitz (Occasional Paper 90); *The Behavior of Income Shares: Selected Theoretical and Empirical Issues* (Studies in Income and Wealth 27); and *Measuring the Nation's Wealth* (Studies in Income and Wealth 29).

Three reports are in press: *Output, Employment, and Productivity in the United States after 1800* (Studies in Income and Wealth 30); *Determinants and Effects of Changes in the Stock of Money, 1875-1960,* by Phillip Cagan; and *Trade Union Membership, 1897-1962,* by Leo Troy (Occasional Paper 92).

Plans for a broad program of studies of productivity, employment, and price levels are described in Part III A. For other studies of economic growth, see section 2 and Juster's report in section 4.

2. NATIONAL INCOME, CONSUMPTION, AND CAPITAL FORMATION

INVESTMENT IN EDUCATION

In December 1964 my book *Human Capital* was published. It contains the theoretical and empirical results of my study of the economic effects of various kinds of human capital, especially education.

Among other things, the book outlines a theory relating human capital to the personal distribution of income, and promises more work to come. To make good on this promise, a more intensive theoretical and empirical investigation of income distributions has been started. The theoretical analysis relates the distribution of earnings to rates of return on human capital and to the distribution of investments in human capital as well as to the distribution of luck and ability.

Rates of return and investments in human capital are in turn related to the degree of equality of opportunity, the functioning of capital markets, the demand for skilled personnel, and other institutional factors. For example, equality of opportunity is said to be greater the more alike are the effective supply curves of investment funds to different persons. The greater the equality of opportunity, therefore, the more is the distribution of investments in human capital dominated by differences in expected rates of return. Since "ability" is essentially defined by these rates, one can conclude that the greater the equality of opportunity, the more is the distribution of investments determined by the distribution of ability.

The theory is developed in such a way as to make the more important influences amenable to empirical analysis. For want of data, however, the empirical analysis relates the distribution of earnings to only one kind of human capital, formal education. The study is focusing on comparisons among geographical areas, specifically states and regions of the United States and different countries; information has already been collected for states and regions, and, is now being obtained for several countries. A preliminary analysis indicates that differences in educational opportunities play an important role in explaining differences among areas in the inequality and skewness of earnings. For example, more than a third of the differences in inequality among states in 1959 is apparently explained either by differences in rates of return or in the degree of inequality in the distribution of education.

Personnel on the project includes Barry Chiswick, who is writing his Ph.D. dissertation on this subject, and Linda Kee, who is providing general research assistance.

GARY S. BECKER

CONSUMER PURCHASE PLANS

This project, which was regarded as completed with the publication of my *Anticipations and Purchases* monograph, has been reactivated on a small scale to permit the analysis of a body of experimental survey data provided by the U.S. Bureau of the Census. One of the main conclusions of the monograph was that surveys of consumer intentions to buy durable goods probably constituted an inefficient and relatively inaccurate way to obtain an estimate of prospective purchase rates for durables, and that a survey of explicit purchase probabilities might well represent an improvement. In July 1964 the Census Bureau reinterviewed a sample of households that had participated the previous week in its regular survey of buying intentions, using an experimental survey designed to provide a measure of the respondent's purchase probability for a list of consumer durables. A further reinterview to determine actual purchases was undertaken in January, roughly six months after both the intentions survey and the probability survey were taken.

The object of this experiment is to contrast the efficiency with which the two surveys—the regular intentions survey and the roughly contemporaneous experimental survey of purchase probabilities—can predict differences in purchase rates among sample households. The only possible source of difference, given the experimental design, lies in the way that respondents react to the alternative survey questions. The regular intentions survey asks, "Do you expect to buy a [car, washing machine . . .] during the next [6, 12] months?" while the experimental probability survey asks, "What are the prospects [chances] that you will buy a [car, washing machine . . .] during the next [6, 12] months?" The intentions question is open-ended, in that the respondent says whatever he thinks appropriate and the interviewer then codes the answer into a classification consisting of definite, probable, maybe, don't know, and no. The probability question must be answered from a list of possible responses; these consist of a 10-through-0 scale accompanied by both descriptive adjectives (10 = certain or almost certain, 0 = no chance or almost no chance) and quantitative equivalents (10 = 99 in 100, 0 = 1 in 100).

The design of the experiment will permit a cross classification of buying intentions with purchase probabilities, enabling us to pinpoint the source as well as the extent of any differences that emerge. Since the experimental survey constitutes an empirical test of a set of propositions already developed at some length in the *Anticipations* monograph, the results should be available quite rapidly—within a few months after the data have been obtained from the Census Bureau.

In addition to facilitating a direct comparison of the alternative surveys, the experiment is designed to permit analysis of the influence on purchases of both the contemporaneous expectations and attitudes of sample households, and of unexpected (wholly or partly unforeseen) changes in their financial circumstances. The hypotheses to be tested here are also developed at length in the *Anticipations* monograph.

Financial support for the project has been provided by a grant from the Automobile Manufacturers Association, Inc.

F. THOMAS JUSTER

The project has been supported by the Maurice and Laura Falk Foundation and by a supplementary grant from the Life Insurance Association of America.

ROGER F. MURRAY

PROJECTIONS OF PRIVATE PENSION PLANS, 1962-82

A revised draft of the manuscript that sets out the projections, explains their derivation, and discusses their implications has been completed. The present version incorporates changes made in response to the suggestions and criticisms of the pension study's advisory committee and other students of the subject. The main consequence has been a proliferation of projections as account was taken of alternative possibilities. The study is concerned particularly with projections of pension funds and annual changes therein, but other projections required in their derivation—coverage, benefits, and beneficiaries—are also of interest in their own right. Projections have been made of private industrial plans in the aggregate and broken down into insured and noninsured, and of the state-local government plans as well.

DANIEL M. HOLLAND

THE IMPACT OF PUBLIC AND PRIVATE PENSION SYSTEMS ON SAVING AND INVESTMENT

We are now engaged in revising the various study papers and the summary of major findings. The process of review by our advisory committee and by the Board of Directors of the National Bureau should be completed this year. Phillip Cagan's study paper on the impact of pensions on aggregate personal saving is now being reviewed by the Board, and the status of Daniel Holland's projections of pension programs in the future is reported below.

PHILANTHROPY IN THE AMERICAN ECONOMY

Our study is approaching completion. A first draft of the manuscript for Chapters 1-7 and 9 is in hand and work has begun on Chapter 8.

The chapters are entitled:
1. Introduction
2. Income of Private Domestic Philanthropy
3. Recipient Institutions of Private Domestic Philanthropy
4. Private Foreign Aid

5. Social Welfare and Public Philanthropy
6. Veterans' Benefits
7. Other Public Domestic Philanthropy: (A) Public Aid, (B) Other Welfare, (C) Health, (D) Free Schools
8. Social Insurance and Public Philanthropy
9. Nonmilitary Foreign Aid
10. Summary and Conclusions

FRANK G. DICKINSON

ESTIMATES OF PRIVATE GIVING

Over the past year my work on two papers, supplementing the report described by Dr. Dickinson, has been proceeding on a part-time basis.

The first deals with the estimates of total private giving. A preliminary manuscript has been revised and updated. In the process additional data sources have been consulted, and the estimates have been refined and made more comparable in concept. The estimates as here presented are therefore somewhat more reliable than those presented in previous reports.

In 1960 the amount of giving from nongovernmental sources to organizations supported in part or in full by such giving was estimated to be in the range of $9.8 to $11.5 billion (Table IV-8). In 1950 total giving was estimated to be from $4.5 to $5.1 billion. This 122 per cent increase in private giving compares to an increase in gross national product, over the same period, of 77 per cent.

This comparison does not include most philanthropic income in kind, such as the services of buildings, laboratories, libraries, and other physical assets acquired through past donations. Were the implicit rental income from these assets to be counted, total 1960 philanthropic income might be increased by a billion or more dollars.

For the 1950's, the total based on data derived from recipient categories ranged between 85 and 88 per cent of that derived from donor categories. Attempts to reconcile the difference have uncovered reasons for discrepancies, but no precise measures of the separate magnitudes involved. Part of the discrepancy arises from differences in concept and definition. Part may arise from the time lag between the initial act of giving and the receipt of the gift by the ultimate donee. Over a period of regular increases in giving, this would make recipient totals consistently lower than donor totals. Another part arises from incomplete coverage of the multitude of recipient organizations and from the fact that some organizations report receipts net of fund-raising and administrative costs. Part may represent overstatements of the religious and charitable deductions claimed on tax returns, which would inflate the estimates based on donors' data.

Recent reports by the Bureau of Labor Statistics on the 1960-61 *Survey of Consumer Expenditures* provide greatly expanded data for the analysis of family giving. It is hoped that the new data will permit me to measure more conclusively the effects on giving of such family characteristics as income, age, occupation, and education.

A second manuscript, on economic aspects of corporation giving, has been read by a staff reading committee and is being revised in the light of the comments received.

RALPH L. NELSON

OTHER STUDIES

Evidences of Long Swings in Aggregate Construction Since the Civil War, by Moses Abramovitz (Occasional Paper 90); *The Flow of Capital Funds in the Postwar Economy,* by Raymond W. Goldsmith; *Research in the Capital Markets,* by the National Bureau's Exploratory Committee on Research in the Capital Markets; and *The Measurement of Corporate Sources and Uses of Funds,* by David Meiselman and Eli Shapiro (Technical Paper 18), were published. Also published

TABLE IV-8

THE COMPOSITION OF PRIVATE GIVING, 1950 AND 1960

(dollars in millions)

Sources (Donors)	1950	1960	Uses (Recipients)	1950	1960
Living donors (persons and families)	4,359	9,183	Religious organizations[a]	1,961	4,550
Bequests	274	951	Private, primary and secondary schools	438	970
Corporations[b]	217	465			
Foundations[c]	150	701	Higher education	447	1,199
Endowment income			Secular health	532	990
Higher education	100	205	Secular welfare	742	1,315
Health and hospitals	10	20	Other	295	790
Total	$5,110	$11,525		$4,415	$9,814

[a] Includes church-supported health and welfare, and excludes parochial schools.
[b] Adjusted for the effect of company-sponsored foundations on the flow of corporation giving.
[c] Excludes the expenditures of company-sponsored foundations.

were Volumes 27, 28, and 29 of Studies in Income and Wealth: *The Behavior of Income Shares: Selected Theoretical and Empirical Issues; Models of Income Determination;* and *Measuring the Nation's Wealth.*

Conferences on Investment Behavior and on Industrial Composition of Income and Product are being arranged (see Part V). For other studies concerned with consumption and investment consult sections 1, 3, and 4.

3. BUSINESS CYCLES

GENERAL STUDIES

It is hoped that arrangements can be made to reprint Arthur F. Burns's lengthy paper on business cycles, prepared for the new *International Encyclopaedia of the Social Sciences,* together with charts and tables setting forth measures of the cyclical behavior of economic time series. Work on the preparation of these statistical materials for publication is under way.

STUDY OF SHORT-TERM ECONOMIC FORECASTING

This project, which is supported by grants to the National Bureau from several industrial companies, has as its main purpose an evaluation of short-term forecasts of economic developments in the United States.

The following manuscripts have reached the first-draft stage and are now in the process of being revised: "An Appraisal of some

Aggregative Short-Term Forecasts," by Victor Zarnowitz; "The Short-Term Forecasting Ability of Econometric Models," by Jon Cunnyngham; and "The 1965 NBER Indicators: An Expanded Analytical Scheme," by Geoffrey H. Moore and Julius Shiskin. Summaries of these three papers were presented at the December 1964 meeting of the American Statistical Association.

Similarly advanced are "Recognition of Cyclical Turning Points," by Rendigs Fels; "On Some Criteria of Evaluation of Forecasts," by Jacob Mincer and Victor Zarnowitz; and "Variable Span Diffusion Indexes: A Tool for Analysis of Current Economic Change," by Geoffrey H. Moore and Julius Shiskin. Rosanne Cole is preparing a draft of a paper on revisions in the official estimates of gross national product and their effects on forecast accuracy.

Our work has benefited greatly from the advice and assistance of many individuals. We cannot list them all here, but must mention in particular the debt we owe to those men and institutions who represent the sources of our forecast materials: without their cooperation, most of the data could not have been assembled and processed. We are especially indebted, also, to Gordon McKinley, McGraw-Hill Publishing Company, Inc., and Daniel B. Suits, University of Michigan, for their helpful comments on the three papers presented at the American Statistical Association meeting.

Fuller accounts of selected parts of the study appear in Part II. The individual reports that follow describe briefly the state of research in other areas covered by the project.

VICTOR ZARNOWITZ

Econometric Model Forecasts

The first report of the NBER study of short-term econometric model forecasting was presented in December at the annual meetings of the American Statistical Association. It analyzed published reports of 46 forecasts of GNP and its major components in the postwar period from econometric models of the United States. The analysis suggests that econometric models have not been able to forecast the *levels* of aggregate economic activity as well as have some general business forecasts. This negative finding is due primarily to the imputation to these models of price movement forecasts which, although included in the published reports, were not usually generated from within the model. In forecasting *changes* in aggregate economic activity which exclude these price movements, econometric models have been about as accurate as the better business forecasts.

In addition to the analysis of published econometric forecasts reported in December, a more comprehensive set of *ex post* forecasts have been computed from the published models. A detailed evaluation of these models is being undertaken to identify factors which promote successful econometric forecasting. The forecasts are designed to provide the standardized structures of classification needed for analyzing the constraints which currently differentiate these forecasting models.

ANNUAL ECONOMETRIC FORECASTS

A comparison of errors in forecasting levels and changes for published annual econometric model forecasts of GNP and six major components is presented in Table IV-9. For each year the forecast values of the annual level and change for that year from the estimated level of the previous base year (usually estimated early in November) have been compared with the actual figures as reported in the first February issue of the *Survey of Current Business* following the year to which the forecast applies. These figures were used in preference to current reports from the Department of Commerce because it was felt that they tend to be more consistent with the predetermined variables which were available at the time of forecast.

Occasionally, several forecasts were made for a particular year with no clear preference of the forecaster, express or implied. In 1958,

TABLE IV-9

ANALYSIS OF ERRORS IN ECONOMETRIC FORECASTS OF
GROSS NATIONAL PRODUCT AND SELECTED COMPONENTS, ANNUALLY, 1953-63
(billions of current dollars)

Year	Model	Total GNP Level	Total GNP Change[a]	Consumption Expenditures Level	Consumption Expenditures Change	Residential Construction Level	Residential Construction Change	Gross Private Investment Level	Gross Private Investment Change	Plant and Equipment Expenditures Level	Plant and Equipment Expenditures Change	Corporate Profits Level	Corporate Profits Change	Inventory Investment Level	Inventory Investment Change
1953	1-A	11.91	−0.89	0.37	−3.14	—	—	1.36	−3.96	—	—	−5.86	0.19	—	—
1954	2-A	28.40	5.20	4.40	0.56	—	—	6.60	0.56	—	—	0.10	5.96	—	—
1955	3-A	−22.37	−20.75	−15.15	−14.85	—	—	−4.57	−2.77	—	—	−7.90	−1.20	—	—
1956	1-B	−12.44	−4.08	−1.36	−3.07	—	—	7.33	7.41	—	—	2.85	7.49	—	—
1957	2-B	0.94	6.40	−0.52	0.33	1.81	1.85	4.33	5.63	0.81	1.34	3.24	6.78	1.80	2.59
1958	3-B	−0.26	8.31	−0.78	−0.89	−4.01	−3.93	11.32	10.97	9.26	9.25	5.40	5.84	6.43	6.03
1959	4-B	−18.65	−11.26	−12.90	−11.90	−3.91	−3.46	−8.67	−6.24	0.87	1.09	0.73	5.19	−5.36	−3.66
1960	5-B	0.53	−7.19	−11.70	−5.64	1.65	1.11	1.64	1.12	1.15	0.76	4.46	3.84	−1.12	−0.90
1961	6-B	−9.24	−3.36	−2.00	−1.75	1.17	1.25	1.80	0.75	0.89	0.71	−0.05	−1.66	−0.30	−1.21
1962	7-B	2.93	0.12	−3.88	0.57	−2.46	−1.77	−4.42	−2.86	−2.62	−2.04	−0.56	−0.28	0.58	0.88
1963	8-B	−2.67	−5.93	−3.66	−0.45	−1.14	−1.14	−5.08	−5.26	−1.45	−1.05	−0.30	0.61	−2.14	−2.60

SUMMARY STATISTICS

Arithmetic mean error		−1.90	−3.04	−4.29	−3.66	−0.98	−0.87	1.06	0.49	1.27	1.44	0.19	2.98	−0.01	0.16
Standard deviation		14.19	8.42	6.21	5.21	2.56	2.34	6.17	5.52	3.80	3.66	4.06	3.47	3.64	3.32
Root mean square error		14.32	8.95	7.54	6.36	2.74	2.49	6.26	5.54	4.01	3.93	4.07	4.57	3.64	3.32

[a]Excludes error of forecast price change.

for example, the data were selected from a group of three distinct forecasts: one taken from the econometric model itself, a second obtained by inserting a single prediction of gross capital formation in place of the investment equation, and a third obtained by assuming about a 5 per cent decline in the level of investment from that of the previous year. Given the discretion involved in selecting the appropriate forecast and observed values, one should regard this table of forecast errors as tentative.

In the table, the figures shown are all expressed in current dollar values, even though the models from which the data derive were largely formulated and the forecasts themselves usually expressed in terms of changes in constant dollar values. A striking result is the lack of relation visible between these econometric models' ability to forecast GNP and their ability to forecast the GNP components. For example, when a model forecasts very well, such as in 1953 and 1962, the corresponding errors in the components are not reduced correspondingly: errors of change in consumption expenditures rank eighth and fourth, respectively, and errors of change in gross private investment rank sixth and fifth, out of a possible eleven. The worst forecast of all (in 1955) did equally badly forecasting consumption expenditures, but did fourth out of eleven in forecasting both gross private investment and corporate profits.

Another result, shown in Table IV-10, is an analysis of how well the forecast directions of change in GNP and its components correspond with the directions of change actually observed. Such an analysis for variables which change direction frequently, such as gross private investment and corporate profits, is a measure of their turning-point correspondence. Since some variables, such as total GNP and consumption expenditures, seldom show any declines on an annual basis, the directions of changes in the rate of change of forecast values are also compared in the table. These differences, represented by Δ^2, may be of some importance because of their relation to business recessions and recoveries.

On this basis, the econometric forecasts of total GNP and plant and equipment expenditures have the best record. However, it should be noted that the forecasts of the latter were often not derived from the set of simultaneously solved equations representing the econometric model. The worst set of forecasts on the basis of turning-point correspondence, as shown in Table IV-10, is the forecasts of residential construction. Their first and second difference forecasts behave in an almost random fashion with respect to the differences actually observed.

Perhaps the single most important contribution econometric models can make to the advancement of the forecasting art is the ability to work back from the final forecast to the initial projections and assumptions concerning the exogenous variables. It is in this way that the consistency of each variable with the others and with the entire system of equations can be exposed to the best analytic power the forecaster can bring to bear. In these econometric models the contribution of each variable entering the forecast will be related to the final forecast of each endogenous variable. Given this information, the effects of autonomous shifts may be calculated; the stability of the final forecasts estimated from the variability of the inputs; and the more sensitive input variables revealed.

AUTOREGRESSIVE EXTRAPOLATION

In pursuit of the newer and more glamorous econometric techniques, it is easy to overlook that the older methods of extrapolation, trend projection, cyclical analysis, and correlation still produce good results for experienced statisticians. In order to gauge the relative forecasting power of current econometric models against these older and proven techniques, we have designed a purely statistical model which incorporates some of these methods in a statistical decision rule structure. The final result, presented in the December paper, is a general form of autoregressive extrapolation.

TABLE IV-10

CORRESPONDENCE OF FORECAST AND ACTUAL DIRECTIONS OF CHANGE IN GROSS NATIONAL PRODUCT AND SELECTED COMPONENTS, ANNUALLY, 1953-63

Variable		53	54	55	56	57	58	59	60	61	62	63	Average Correspondence (per cent)
Total GNP	Δ	+	+	+	+	+	−	+	+	+	+	+	91
	Δ^2	+	+	+	−	+	+	+	+	+	+	+	80
Consumption expenditures	Δ	+	+	+	+	+	+	+	+	+	+	+	100
	Δ^2	+	−	−	+	−	+	+	−	+	+	+	60
Residential construction	Δ			+		−	−	+	−	+	+	+	57
	Δ^2			+	−	+	−	+	+	+	−	+	50
Gross private investment	Δ	−	+	+	+	−	−	+	+	+	+	+	73
	Δ^2	+	+	+	−	+	+	+	+	+	+	+	90
Plant and equipment expenditures	Δ					+	−	+	+	+	+	+	85
	Δ^2					+	+	+	+	+	+	+	100
Corporate profits	Δ	+	+	+	−	−	−	+	−	+	+	+	64
	Δ^2	+	+	+	+	+	+	+	+	−	+	+	90
Inventory investment	Δ					+	−	+	+	+	+	−	72
	Δ^2					−	+	+	+	+	−	−	67

NOTE: Δ = Correspondence of directions of change; Δ^2 = Correspondence of directions of change in rate of change; + = Positive correspondence; − = Inverse correspondence.

This yardstick of forecasting performance may be thought of as the extrapolation of a nonstationary stochastic process consisting of three components: a systematic component represented by a linear combination of quantities over time, a linear autoregressive and moving average component measuring the significance of the interaction of the economic indicator with its recent history at a point in time, and a random component. One measure of the forecasting ability of the econometric models analyzed in this study will be their performance relative to this autoregressive forecasting model.

JON CUNNYNGHAM

RECOGNITION OF CYCLICAL TURNING POINTS

For the eight business cycle peaks and troughs from 1948 through 1961, I have studied reports on the business outlook in more than a dozen periodical business and financial publications. The purpose was to appraise the published record with respect to early warning and prompt confirmation of cyclical turning points. I have written a report for consideration as an Occasional Paper.

In an interval beginning some time before a cyclical peak or trough and extending as much as six months after it, there is a more or less regular pattern in reports on the business outlook as analysts become increasingly aware of first the possibility, then the probability, and finally the certainty of a turning point. Confirmation comes between three and six months after the peak or trough.

Geoffrey Moore, writing in 1950 about "the usual lag in recognizing revivals or recessions *that have already begun,*" said that "this lag is clearly not negligible. If the user of statistical indicators could do no better than recognize contemporaneously the turns in general economic activity denoted by our reference dates,

he would have a better record than most of his fellows."[1] My study confirms Moore's observation. To "forecast" turning points regularly with no more than a zero lead would be to exceed the general run of publications I have studied.

Since World War II, anticipation of upturns has been better than of downturns. Forecasters have generally expected each contraction to be short, and to be milder than such major contractions of the past as 1920-21, 1929-33, and 1937-38. Although they were not able to pinpoint when the trough would come, they were basically right.

Forecasts, especially those based on national income analysis, can go badly astray as a result of faulty estimates of a single statistical series. In 1947, a poor seasonal adjustment of industrial production led to false confirmation of a downturn. In 1957, the preliminary estimate of inventory investment for the first quarter had the wrong sign, leading some forecasters to expect continued cyclical expansion instead of the downturn that actually occurred.

The study tends to confirm the value of business cycle indicators. Although they have sometimes given false signals, at times (notably in 1957) the indicators have enabled those forecasters who relied on them to recognize the turning point faster than anyone else.

RENDIGS FELS

BUSINESS CYCLE INDICATORS

A comprehensive review of the NBER cyclical indicators, covering conventional economic time series and diffusion indexes, was carried out during the past year.

The first list of NBER indicators was issued

---

[1] *Statistical Indicators of Cyclical Revivals and Recessions,* Occasional Paper 31, New York, NBER, 1950, p. 76.

in 1938. The list was revised in 1950 and again in 1960. Periodic revisions are required because of the appearance of new economic time series, new findings of business cycle research, and the changing structure of the American economy. About 115 series were covered in the present review, including those that came out well in previous studies and other series that appear promising for this purpose. This review of the indicators was concerned with two aspects of their use: (1) quality of the series as cyclical indicators and (2) organization and classification. It is limited to the role of economic time series as business cycle indicators, and may not be relevant to their other uses.

The current review has extended the use of explicit criteria and objective standards employed by Mitchell, Burns, and Moore in establishing previous lists. This has been accomplished by a plan for assigning scores to each series, within a range of 0 to 100. The scoring of each series reflects our desire to make as explicit as possible the criteria for selecting indicators, as well as to increase the amount of information available to the user to aid in evaluating the current behavior of the indicators.

The scoring plan includes six major elements: (1) economic significance, (2) statistical adequacy, (3) historical conformity to business cycles, (4) cyclical timing record, (5) smoothness, and (6) promptness of publication. Subclassifications are included under most of these elements, with some twenty different properties of series being rated in all. This list of properties provides a view of the many different considerations relevant to an appraisal of the value of a statistical series for current business cycle analysis.

In classifying indicators into groups useful for purposes of business cycle analysis, it is desirable to take account of both their economic interrelationships and their cyclical behavior. Consideration therefore has been given to various criteria for such a classification, including type of economic process, consistency of conformity to business cycles, and timing at business cycle peaks and troughs. The advantages of providing both a relatively short list of indicators as well as a much longer list have also been considered.

Our tentative conclusions on these points are:

1. To use as a major principle of classification the fourfold grouping: Leading, Roughly Coincident, Lagging, and Unclassified by Cyclical Timing. The first three categories take into account timing at both peaks and troughs, but within them we plan to distinguish peak from trough timing where they are significantly different. The fourth category includes economic activities important for business cycles, but which have displayed a less regular relation to them.

2. To use as a secondary principle of classification the type of economic process represented by the series, having in mind particularly the processes that are important for business cycle analysis. The following nine categories have been selected: employment and unemployment; production, income, and trade; fixed capital investment; inventories; prices and costs; money and credit; foreign trade and payments; federal government activity; production and prices in other countries.

3. To develop both a short list of about 25 indicators as well as a longer list of 75 to 100. The short list would contain little duplication and would be convenient for summarization. The long list would fill more of the needs of the analyst.

A paper incorporating these ideas, "The 1965 NBER Indicators—An Expanded Analytical Scheme," was presented at the December 1964 meetings of the American Statistical Association. A revised draft, which will include the new list and classification, is being prepared.

Our review of diffusion indexes considered existing knowledge of their properties and investigated the effects of computing diffusion indexes over long spans. A paper, "Variable Span Diffusion Indexes—A Tool for the Analysis of Economic Change," is being prepared.

(An initial draft was presented at the April 1964 meeting of the New York Chapter of the American Statistical Association.)

The new findings concern the relative advantages of diffusion indexes computed over short and long spans, and of cumulated diffusion indexes and moving averages. As a result of this work, a new collection and arrangement of diffusion indexes was introduced in the Department of Commerce monthly publication, *Business Cycle Developments*. A pair of diffusion indexes is shown for each economic activity, one long-span (six or nine months depending upon irregularity) and one short-span (one month or quarter). The long-span index is smoother and portrays cyclical movements more clearly. However, it does not show changes that have taken place within the span. While the short-span indexes are usually very erratic, they reveal widespread changes promptly. Since such changes often occur around cyclical turning points, the one-month indexes will sometimes give an earlier and more precise indication of a cyclical turning point than the corresponding longer-term index.

JULIUS SHISKIN
GEOFFREY H. MOORE

GNP REVISIONS AND FORECASTING ACCURACY

The poor quality of the available data is often cited as one of the sources of error in forecasts of business conditions. This part of the forecasting study appraises one aspect of the quality of the data used in forecasts of future values of gross national product: the accuracy, as indicated by successive revisions, of the provisional estimates of GNP.

The provisional estimates are those values of quarterly GNP which are available one or two months after the close of the quarter covered. They are estimates of the latest levels of GNP which are known to the forecaster at the time he makes his forecasts. Typically, they are used to form the base of his forecasts and, to the extent that they are extrapolations of past changes in GNP, his forecasts of change. Shortcomings in the provisional estimates are thus likely to be transferred to the forecasts.

Estimates of such an aggregate as GNP call on a variety of data sources. Since few of these sources were initially developed as parts of a reporting system designed for estimating current GNP, not all of the data relevant to the period covered are available in time to be incorporated in the first estimates. As new data become available, the initial estimates of a given quarter are periodically revised.

The provisional estimates are themselves a type of forecast in that they are based on only partial information. As might be expected, the revisions of these estimates share many of the characteristics of bona fide forecast errors. The revisions indicate that the provisional estimates of quarterly GNP in the postwar period have been too low, on the average. Further, the magnitude of the revisions increases as the span of months from first to revised estimate increases. That is, new data relevant to the estimate of a given quarter continue to become available some three years (or more) after the time the provisional estimate of GNP was published. For the period studied, 1947-61, data available approximately one year later indicate that the provisional estimates of quarterly GNP averaged $3 billion too low, after two years averaged $3.7 billion too low, and after three years the new data showed them to be an average of $4 billion too low. Finally, as Zarnowitz finds for errors of bona fide forecasts, the variability about the average is related to the cyclical characteristics of the quarter for which GNP was estimated. The average upward revision of the provisional estimates was greatest during the first year of a business cycle expansion ($5.5 billion), somewhat less during later expansion ($3.9 billion), and least during periods of contraction ($2.5 billion).

Unlike forecasts, which Zarnowitz finds underestimate change, the first available estimates of peak-to-trough change have substantially exaggerated the severity of the decline in GNP during each of the four postwar contractions. In every case, overestimates of the decline were the result of underestimating the rise in personal consumption expenditures and overestimating the decline in gross private domestic investment (particularly the change in business inventories).

The revisions of the provisional estimates show the difficulty of measuring GNP on a current basis and therefore provide some notion of tolerable forecast error. The periods most difficult to measure are likely to be those which are also difficult to forecast. Generally, it is suggested that forecasts of GNP should be compared with the first estimates available rather than the values as they appear today, because the forecaster should not be held responsible for the revisions of the estimates which will occur in the future. This procedure only partly eliminates the effects of the revisions (errors in the provisional estimates) on forecast accuracy. In addition, errors (as indicated by subsequent revisions) in the data available at the time forecasts are made are likely to be incorporated in the forecasts. How much these errors influence the forecasts depends on the autoregressive properties of GNP and the extent the forecaster relies on them. Some attempts have been made to estimate the effect on forecast accuracy of using the poorer-quality data available at the time forecasts are made.

The revisions of the provisional estimates of the major GNP components have also been reviewed. Future work on this part of the project includes an analysis of the consequences of this type of measurement error for estimates of the parameters of some single-equation models which include GNP or its major components as variables, and for the accuracy of the forecasts of these models. In addition, it is hoped that the final report will include recommendations for improving the quality of the provisional estimates of GNP.

ROSANNE COLE

STATISTICAL INDICATORS

A review and evaluation of the NBER list of business cycle indicators was carried out, as reported under the study of short-term economic forecasting.

Among the indicators constructed or investigated during the year, two that appear to be the most useful are the following:

1. A monthly index of profit margins and total profits in manufacturing. The index of margins was constructed by adjusting the ratio of wholesale prices to labor cost per unit of output (series 17 in *Business Cycle Developments*) so that its cyclical amplitude approximates that of profits per dollar of sales of manufacturing corporations (series 18 in *BCD*). This was done by a simple mathematical formula. The monthly index of margins was multiplied by a monthly index of manufacturing sales (Department of Commerce) to obtain the index of profits. Despite differences in coverage and concept, the monthly index corresponds fairly closely with the quarterly data on profits of manufacturing corporations (Federal Trade and Securities and Exchange Commissions). The monthly figures can be kept more nearly up to date, and the separate effects of changes in output per man-hour, hourly compensation, wholesale prices, and sales can be observed. This is not possible with the quarterly data derived from financial reports.

2. A quarterly index of labor cost per unit of real corporate gross product (series 68 in *BCD*). This index, covering the entire corporate sector, is more comprehensive than the monthly index of unit labor cost in manufacturing (series 62 in *BCD*), and it is to a large extent statistically independent of the latter. Hence it provides another observation on the movement of this important factor. By omitting agriculture and other unincorporated business, private households, and government, a considerable improvement in the statistical adequacy of the data is secured as compared with the previously published index of labor cost per unit of real gross national product.

GEOFFREY H. MOORE

FLUCTUATION IN STOCKS OF PURCHASED MATERIALS ON HAND AND ON ORDER

Eight chapters of the manuscript have been read by a staff committee. These pages start with an analysis of the functions that inventories serve in business organizations and examine the behavior, as evidenced in data for durable goods manufacturers and department stores, of stocks of purchased materials both on hand and on order and their sum, which we term "ownership." The final chapter of the main body of the work turns to causal explanation, combining two sources of information: business practice or management expertise and time series.

The first source says that stocks do not need to rise as much as sales rise, and that they may respond to shifts in a wide variety of costs (opportunity costs). The second source, the time series, says that stocks on hand actually rise faster than sales about half the time that sales are in rising specific cycle phase, times when the rise in stocks is likely to be intentional. During business cycle expansions from 1948 to 1961, specific cycles in the stock-sales ratios were in rising phase (stocks rising faster than sales) 64 per cent of the months covered for durable-goods manufacturers and 63 per cent for department stores.

To understand this pattern of behavior of stocks on hand, it is necessary to look at the behavior of materials stocks both on hand and on order. Two major sets of influences are at work. The first is demand, as evidenced by retailers' sales or manufacturers' shipments, and, particularly, their rates of change. The second is change in the one set of opportunity costs that can be traced: actual and expected conditions in the markets in which materials or stock in trade are purchased. These costs reflect conditions of supply and its interaction with demand. The first set of influences, sales, seems strongly responsible for the routine timing and the second for the extent and occasional timing of changes in stocks on hand and on order. The evidence of these two major influences is instructively different for the two sorts of enterprises, retail stores and manufacturers, and for the two sorts of stocks (on hand and on order).

For department stores, for which the enforcement of sharply defined stock objectives must carry high management priority, the evidence is in accord with the following grossly simplified story: Retailers buy to achieve an end-of-month inventory objective based on recognized seasonal patterns of sales over the purchasing horizon (the "season"), expected sales for the month, and a judgment about delivery (or price) conditions during the "season." Sales expectations rely heavily on sales of the recent past or corresponding months of the previous year.

If sales turn out to be higher than expected, merchants tend to do three things: (1) place "at once" orders to restore stocks (drawn down by the higher sales) to the desired level very promptly; (2) if the higher sales are not attributed to an ephemeral cause, they place more advance orders to revise the pattern of build-up of stock in line with changed sales expectations; (3) they may place additional advance orders in expectation of market tightness.

Because of the speed with which it operates, device 1 largely erases in end-of-month statistics the inverse impact on stocks of the rate of change in sales. The impact of devices 2 and 3 appears in the lagging correspondence between fluctuations in the rate of change in sales and in stocks (inventory investment); they are in like phase 81 per cent of the postwar months after allowing for a three-month lag of stocks. But the impact can be seen more sharply in the synchronous correspondence between the rate of change in sales and in materials ownership (stocks both on hand and on order), for which 84 per cent of months are in like phase. (A notion of the meaning of this figure is suggested by the fact that since twelve turns occur in the 186 months, if all were matched, an average deviation of no more than two and one half months would be implied.) But though the rate of change in sales goes a long way toward explaining the timing of stock changes, factors 2 and 3 also occasionally influence the timing of turns and usually influence the amplitude of fluctuation. This is greater than that of sales, whereas an efficient sales link would cause it to be smaller. The evidence takes many forms; for example, the ratio of ownership to sales is in rising phase 70 per cent of the months when sales are rising.

Finally, 1, 2, and 3 are all reflected in the association between new orders proper and change in sales. All turns, twelve, are matched and six, five of which are troughs, are virtually synchronous (within plus or minus one month). At peaks, new orders tend to turn down two or three months after sales have stopped rising at an increasing rate. However, on two occasions the lag was quite long and these, according to the data collected by the Chicago Purchasing Agents Association, were both times when markets were unusually tight. The one substantial lag at a trough also occurred (late in 1953) when slackness was sharply evident.

The net result is that new orders lead sales by substantial intervals and have about twice their amplitude of fluctuation. Thereby they convey a cyclical whip and acceleration to the demand at earlier stages of production relative to that of the consumer. New orders placed by department stores usually turn *earlier* than new orders received by all durables goods manufacturers. For the ten turns marked since 1947 in both series, department store orders lead in seven cases, lag in two, and synchronize in one.

Space does not permit a sketch of the equivalent explanation for materials buying by durable goods manufacturers. Suffice it to say that the twofold influence of sales and market conditions is evident, though they have quite different forms and relative importance.

Manufacturers are not willing to pay the opportunity cost of keeping materials stocks in close conformity to a precise sales-linked objective in the first instance. For this reason, and perhaps also because of the character of the objective, changes in sales and in stocks have an inverse association. However, manufacturers do respond to the presence of too much or too little stock, defined very crudely as materials that represent more and less, respectively, than about one month's supply. The stock-sales ratio, then, is the link between the rate of change in sales and new buying of materials. From 1948 on, all ten turns in the stock-sales ratio and in new orders placed for materials are matched inversely. Six of these matched turns are within two months of one another, but in 1948, 1951, and 1956 new orders continued to rise for five months or more after the stock-sales ratio had reached a trough (i.e., stock deficiencies had started to subside). These were just the occasions in which spot-market prices of metals were rising rapidly to unusual highs. The lag at the 1949 trough occurred also at exactly the time when the most abrupt postwar drop in these prices was underway. On some of these occasions, though not all, new orders for final products were also rising (or falling).

Market expectations, then, on several occasions were important determinants of the time when reversals in previous "trends" in buying occurred. But for durable goods manufacturers far more than for department stores, they regularly influence the amount of materials stocks held on hand and particularly on order; for this there are good and sufficient reasons. Fluctuation in the stocks on order (and also in the total) are large and have a close association with an entirely independent source of information on market conditions developed by the Chicago Purchasing Agents Association. I attribute a not inconsiderable part of the fact that increases in stocks were so moderate during the expansion starting in 1961 to the absence, at least until 1964, of expectation of market tightness. This does not deny that control techniques associated with computerization also helped to validate the sales-linked stock objectives. These would in any event tend to dominate, in the absence of worry about lengthening delivery periods or other shifts in opportunity costs of stock (such as the labor cost of flexible production schedules).

These findings seem to bear out the hunch with which the study started: Examination of materials stock on order, viewed along with materials stock on hand, can contribute much to the understanding of the process of stock accumulation and purchasing. If this analysis is correct, the provision of statistics for stocks on order, classified by industry placing the order, warrants a status equal to that accorded the provision of data for stocks on hand. The recent discontinuance of the department store data discussed above was a serious retrogression from this point of view, and I hope it will not prove permanent.

In the wake of the findings here mentioned, along with many others, the usual unanswered questions bubble and churn. For one thing, the study lives in a world of orders in which an explanation of production in terms of new orders is vacuous unless changes in orders themselves are explained. In this world, an insistent fact is the lead of orders placed by the department stores relative to consumer buying, and the fact that those orders, if anything, turn earlier than those for durable goods. This lead of department store orders, in which rates of change in sales as well as market expectations seem to play an important part, raises a question whether the role of capital formation in bringing on business reversals is really paramount. At the same time, it suggests that a deeper understanding of factors that influence the pace of economic change and its governance throughout business expansion might have a bearing on that important question, how to promote long-lived expansion by means other than stiff-arming downturns by fiscal measures.

The study also lives in a world of expectations. The fact that expectations about market conditions ebb and flow, and their apparent association with changes in demand as well as with conditions of supply, raises questions about how these waves in sentiment and related buying come about. Obviously it involves a process which feeds upon itself. But does it also pack an inherent reciprocating mechanism? How? The concluding section of this study touches on these matters.

RUTH P. MACK

LABOR TURNOVER

Two sections of a report on the cyclical behavior of labor turnover, those dealing with cyclical conformity and timing, have been completed, and a third section, on amplitudes, is in preparation. One of the most interesting findings pertains to the consistently long leads of accession rates (gross accessions, net accessions, new hires) at business cycle peaks. During the postwar period these leads were always longer than those of new orders for durables, and their extraordinary length may be associated with the fact that the first phase of recovery in general business activity usually shows the sharpest rise. The subsequent deceleration is reflected in a decrease of the rate of addition to the number employed and in a decline of accession rates. Leads of accession rates before business cycle troughs are also long relative to leads of other activities. However, the leads are not as long as at peaks, partly because of the shorter duration of contractions.

In the course of our work on labor turnover, we had occasion to study Bureau of Employment Security data on job openings received, placements, job openings pending, and job openings canceled. Chart IV-1 illustrates, for the 1958-61 cycle, how these measures are related to one another. Perhaps its most interesting aspect is the small size of the stock of job openings pending, relative to the flow of job openings received. The stock-to-flow ratio is about one third. By contrast, the corresponding ratio of insured unemployment to the flow of intitial claims for unemployment insurance is approximately three to one. This implies that the average duration of a job opening is one third of one month, while the average duration of insured unemployment is three months. However, these findings for job openings pending at employment offices cannot be readily transferred to job vacancies in the economy at large, since only a small fraction of all job vacancies but a very large fraction of all job seekers are registered at employment offices. This makes the filling of job openings at employment offices relatively easy and the stock of openings pending rela-

CHART IV-1

Components of Job Openings Pending, 1958-61

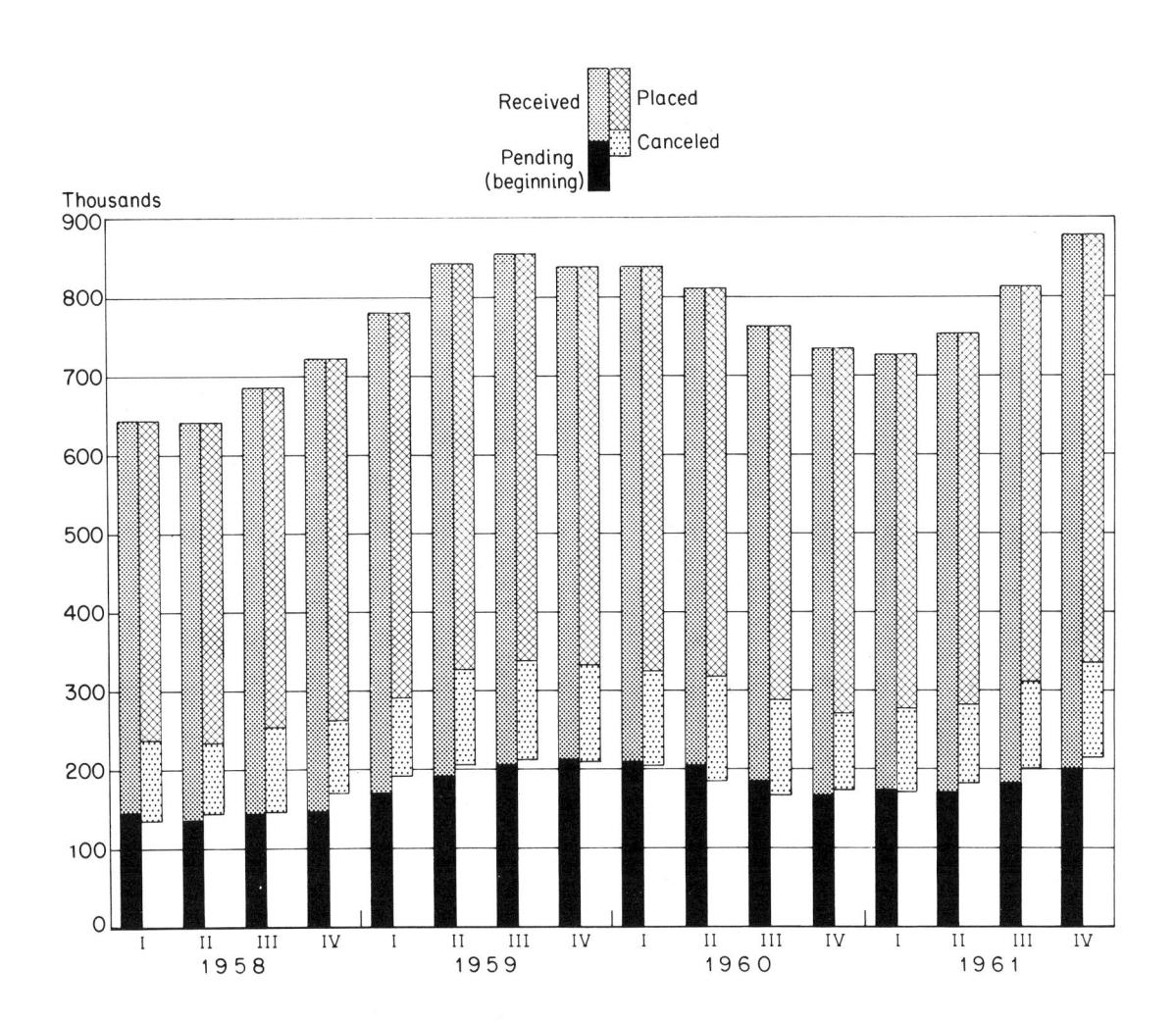

tively low. A paper dealing with these and other measures of labor demand, entitled "Job Openings and Help-Wanted Advertising as Measures of Cyclical Fluctuations in Unfilled Demand for Labor," was prepared for the Conference on Measurement and Interpretation of Job Vacancies.

CHARLOTTE BOSCHAN

MONEY AND BANKING

Work on "Trends and Cycles in the Stock of Money" is proceeding along lines described in last year's Annual Report. There are no substantive results as yet to report on the statistical investigations that are under way.

MILTON FRIEDMAN
ANNA J. SCHWARTZ

SOURCE BOOK OF STATISTICS RELATING TO INVESTMENT

This source book is a compilation of the principal monthly, quarterly, and annual time series on fixed investment in the United States. Its preparation has been supported by a grant from the National Science Foundation.

The National Bureau's collection of historical data on investment forms the main basis of the source book, but it has been necessary to bring up to date or revise most of the series, and many new ones have been added.

All the data published will be accompanied by descriptions of sources and methods of compilation. For monthly and quarterly series, seasonally adjusted as well as original data will be presented, and summary measures of cyclical behavior will be given for some of the more important categories of investment.

Work during the past year has been concentrated on series pertaining to construction activity. Almost one hundred monthly and quarterly series in this area have been compiled and most have been seasonally adjusted. The National Bureau's cyclical analysis is being completed for a selection of these, and the whole group is being prepared for IBM printing. In addition, more than sixty annual construction series are included in the collection.

Descriptions of sources and methods have been prepared for almost all of the monthly and annual series on construction. These, together with the data described above, will form the first installment of the source book, to be completed in 1965.

ROBERT E. LIPSEY
DORIS PRESTON

ELECTRONIC COMPUTER APPLICATIONS

Progress was made on a proposed Technical Paper dealing with the application of electronic computers to different aspects of business cycle analysis. A draft of the part relating to the standard National Bureau analysis is far advanced.

In the field of program development, we wrote a program computing binomial distributions, provided a subroutine for ranking observations, and made numerous improvements in existing programs. Also, we modified the general Data Processing and Multiple Regression Program of the International Monetary Fund to suit our needs, added to our inventory of working programs the Generalized Stepwise Linear Regression Program written by Jon Cunnyngham, and adapted the Bureau of the Census program for computing diffusion indexes. During the past year, the needs for special-purpose programs were more pressing than those for new general-purpose ones, although the existing general programs were used extensively. We wrote special-purpose programs for various NBER studies, including C. Harry Kahn's on the tax treatment of fluctuating incomes, H. G. Georgiadis' on international trade, Victor R. Fuchs's on productivity in the service industries, George R. Morrison's on corporate bond and stock financing, and Jack M. Guttentag's on mortgage interest rates.

We have a considerable backlog of programs which we hope to write during the current year, if time permits. Among the more important ones are two approaches to the determination of cyclical turning points. One, devised by Milton Friedman, is based on the minimization of variances; the other is more closely related to currently used National Bureau methods.

The use of electronic data processing in the National Bureau has expanded rapidly. There were scarcely any studies this past year that did not use electronic computing in one form or another, and some studies involved massive use of data processing and analysis. Altogether, the computer resources available to us are being heavily utilized.

The activities of the electronic computing unit are being supported by a grant from the International Business Machines Corporation as well as by general funds of the National Bureau.

GERHARD BRY
CHARLOTTE BOSCHAN

OTHER STUDIES

A paperback reprint of Chapter 7 of Friedman and Schwartz' *Monetary History,* entitled *The Great Contraction, 1929-33,* was published by Princeton University Press.

Reuben A. Kessel's *The Cyclical Behavior of the Term Structure of Interest Rates* (Occasional Paper 91) and *Models of Income Determination* (Studies in Income and Wealth 28) were published. Thor Hultgren's *Cost, Prices, and Profits: Their Cyclical Relations;* Phillip Cagan's *Determinants and Effects of Changes in the Stock of Money, 1875-1960;* and Philip Klein's *Financial Adjustments to Unemployment* (Occasional Paper 93) are in press. Victor Zarnowitz' manuscript, "Orders and Production in Manufacturing Industries: A Cyclical Analysis," is nearing completion.

A conference on Measurement and Interpretation of Job Vacancies was held in February 1965 (see Part V). Other studies concerned with aspects of business cycles are reported by Cagan, Morrison, Juster, and Earley in section 4 and by Mintz in section 5.

4. FINANCIAL INSTITUTIONS AND PROCESSES

INTEREST RATES

This study, undertaken with the aid of grants from the Life Insurance Association of America, is concerned with the behavior, determinants, and effects of interest rates. Joseph W. Conard, who died on April 5, 1965, had chief responsibility for the planning and direction of the project. He had virtually completed a summary report on the study as a whole, entitled "The Behavior of Interest Rates: A Progress Report," and it will shortly be ready for Board review. Revision of another manuscript by Conard, "Yield Differentials Between Newly Issued and Seasoned Securities," is nearly completed and will be carried out by William H. Brown, Jr., and others on the project staff.

Jack M. Guttentag has been appointed director of the project. His own areas of interest, as well as other studies in progress, are described separately below. In addition, two other studies are under way. William H. Brown, Jr., with the assistance of Stanley Diller, is investigating seasonal variations in interest rates, their measurement, and their determinants. F. Thomas Juster has begun an exploratory study of the effects of interest rates on economic activity, with a view to developing plans for new work on this subject. Other studies in progress are described separately below.

The study is benefiting from the advice and assistance of an advisory committee whose members are W. Braddock Hickman (chairman), Federal Reserve Bank of Cleveland; Julian D. Anthony, Hartford Life Insurance Company; Daniel H. Brill, Board of Governors of the Federal Reserve System; Lester V. Chandler, Princeton University; George T. Conklin, Jr., The Guardian Life Insurance Company of America; Milton Friedman, University of Chicago; Raymond W. Goldsmith, National Bureau of Economic Research; Sidney Homer, Salomon Brothers & Hutzler; Norris Johnson, First National City Bank of New York; Robert G. Link, Federal Reserve Bank of New York; Roger F. Murray, National Bureau of Economic Research; James J. O'Leary, Life Insurance Association of America; Roy L. Reierson, Bankers Trust Company; Eli Shapiro, Harvard University; Henry C. Wallich, Yale University; and C. Richard Youngdahl, Aubrey G. Lanston and Company. W. A. Clarke was a member of the committee until his death on February 8, 1965.

The Mortgage Market

The study of the mortgage market is proceeding along two fronts: a time series study that is compiling new historical data from the records of life insurance companies and perhaps other lenders, and a cross-section study of the principal factors influencing the structure of mortgage yields, which employs existing data provided by the Federal Reserve Bank of Chicago and other sources.

The task of compiling time series on residential mortgage yields and terms for the period January 1951–June 1963 is completed except for tabulation. Last-minute changes in our computer program have delayed the tabulations, but they should be available soon. The series will cover FHA, VA, and conventional loans, separately as well as combined, and some will carry nine-region and four-region breaks. Among the loan characteristics for which monthly and quarterly averages as well as standard deviations will be computed are contract rate, net discount, effective rate, effective rate net of service fee (for loans acquired through correspondents only), term to maturity, loan-value ratio, and loan size.

During the summer we began to collect data on "nonresidential" mortgages, which include loans secured by multiple-family residential structures. Data are being provided by fifteen life insurance companies active in this field. Information broadly comparable to that obtained on residential loans is being drawn for every nonresidential loan authorized by these companies since 1951. (For the residential series, in contrast, we drew a sample of loans from participating companies, except for two benchmark months for which coverage was complete.) In addition, for loans authorized during each of three separate quarters during the period, we are obtaining a wider range of information covering borrower characteristics. These data should be particularly valuable for cross-section analysis. Roughly half of the data-collecting job was completed during the summer. The balance is to be completed by this spring.

In the cross-section study of yield determinants, a new approach is being employed to study the problem of risk. This method focuses on two measures which are designed to capture "borrower risk" and "property risk" respectively. Borrower risk refers to the probability that the borrower will be unable to service the loan, and it is measured by the ratio of his mortgage payment to his income. Property risk refers to the probability that the value of the underlying property will, at some time over its life, fall below the outstanding loan balance, thus encouraging default and increasing loss to the lender if default occurs. Property risk is measured by the ratio of outstanding loan balance after five years to the initial property value. Property risk is thus influenced by both the original loan-value ratio and the maturity. The mortgage payment-income and balance-value ratios are calculated on the basis of a standardized contract rate, rather than the actual contract rate on individual transactions. This avoids the difficulty of two-way causation between the contract rate and the risk measures.

The main reason for the new procedure is to avoid some serious problems involved in analyzing the rate effect of the loan maturity. The loan maturity affects both property risk and borrower risk, but in divergent ways. A longer maturity, for example, reduces the borrower's monthly mortgage payment, thus raising the income coverage and reducing borrower risk. However, a mortgage of longer maturity also implies a smaller accumulated repayment of principal after any given period and therefore a smaller margin between outstanding debt and property value, which raises property risk. In addition, the maturity is related to the liquidity of the mortgage. In the new procedure the risk effects of the maturity are automatically incorporated in the two calculated measures and any residual influence of maturity on rate can be ascribed to liquidity effects.

I expect to have a draft of a Technical Paper describing the time series ready by summer, and a progress report on cross-section studies later in the year.

JACK M. GUTTENTAG

YIELDS ON DIRECT PLACEMENTS

The prime purposes of this study have been (1) to construct series, homogeneous through time, on yields on direct placements, 1951-61, and (2) to ascertain whether, over the same period, the underlying characteristics of direct placements have changed and, if so, in which direction and to what extent. The major portion of the support for the study has come from the Life Insurance Association of America. Supplementary support has been provided by the Graduate School of Business Administration and the Research Computation Center, University of North Carolina, and the Institut pour l'Etude des Methodes de Direction de l'Entreprise (IMEDE), Lausanne, Switzerland.

In general, cross-section regression analysis has been used to isolate those characteristics of direct placements which tend to be responsible, at a given time, for differences in yield. From these results two types of quarterly yield series have been constructed: series based on original observations cross-classified by the more significant variables, and series computed from the quarterly regression equations. Both types have already been constructed for industrials and utilities. Construction of a third type of series for both industrials and utilities is under way, namely, a computed series based on *weighted averages* of the quarterly cross-section regression coefficients. Use of weighted-average regression coefficients should, in principle at least, eliminate the effect of the sampling error present in the original cross-section coefficients.

After the cross-classified series were completed, a preliminary comparison was made between yields on high-grade direct placements and yields (to the issuer) on comparable public offerings. This comparison suggested that yields on direct placements tend to be somewhat higher than yields on public offerings. This finding should be regarded with caution, however, because we do not yet know whether the issues compared are, in fact, strictly comparable in every essential respect. And, in any case, for high-grade issues, i.e., for those which clearly have unobstructed access for either market, any yield differential in favor of public offerings would merely represent the price issuers have shown themselves willing to pay to avoid the uncertainty and other tribulations of the public market.

With respect to public utilities, the significant variables are as follows: earnings before interest and taxes, times charges earned, total capitalization, average term, type of security, industrial class, size of issue, debt-equity ratio, maturity, and years nonrefundable.

Drafts of the following chapters for the report on the study have been completed, except for parts of Chapter VII. The final draft is expected to be finished before July.

  I. Introduction and Summary of Findings
  II. Methodology
  III. Yields on Industrials
  IV. Yields on Public Utilities
  V. Yields on Direct Placements compared with Yields on Public Offerings
  VI. The Changing Characteristics of Direct Placements
  VII. Conclusions and Suggestions for Further Research

AVERY B. COHAN

CYCLICAL BEHAVIOR OF INTEREST RATES

A paper analyzing changes in cyclical behavior since 1878 is being revised and should be ready soon for submission to the Board. The main finding is that cycles in interest rates have tended to have greater amplitude over time and shorter timing lags behind business cycles. At recent turning points, some rates even turn before business activity does. A section of this paper explores the effect of variations in growth of the money stock on cycles in interest rates. The analysis suggests that those variations help explain the changes in cyclical behavior of interest rates.

I am presently extending the study of monetary factors to analyze the separate effects of bank loans and investments on interest rates, and to examine the causal relation between banks' free reserves and interest rates.

The main direction of future work on the cyclical behavior of rates has not been definitely settled, but the work is expected to bring in the role of nonbank financial institutions and government debt issues, and to examine patterns in the sequence of turning points among various interest rates, in order to shed light on how factors affecting capital markets influence business investment.

PHILLIP CAGAN

TRENDS AND CYCLES IN CORPORATE BOND AND STOCK FINANCING

The objectives of this study are threefold: first, to conduct a cyclical analysis of fluctuations in corporate debt and equity financing for the period 1900-1963; second, to evaluate the influence of stock and bond yield variations as determinants of cyclical patterns in the debt-equity structure of financing; third, to estimate the secular trends in the structure of corporate financing and assess the factors contributing to these trends. Support is being provided under the grant by the Alfred P. Sloan Foundation for the Research Fellow program.

Currently in progress are the first two stages, which extend to the postwar period W. Braddock Hickman's study of the cyclical behavior of bond and stock financing (Chapter 3 of *The Volume of Corporate Bond Financing since 1900*). Reference cycle and specific cycle analyses of Hickman's data for the period 1900-1943 are being revised to incorporate improvements in seasonal adjustment techniques, changes in reference cycle dating, and use of yield series as alternatives to security price series. The basic financing series being examined are Hickman's monthly corporate bond offerings, extinguishments, and net change in outstanding bonds; the SEC's quarterly new corporate issues, retirements, and net cash change; and the SEC and the *Commercial and Financial Chronicle* monthly series on common and preferred stock offerings. An attempt will be made to develop monthly or quarterly refundings series covering most of the time span of the study. Industry detail will be limited to three broad groups: industrials, railroads, and public utilities.

Seasonal adjustment of these corporate financing data presents difficulties because the unadjusted series display extremely large random variations. It turns out that an adaptation of existing "additive" and "multiplicative" adjustments, in order to select from them minimal seasonal adjustments, produces satisfactory results. A compilation of the seasonally adjusted corporate financing series and a description of the new minimum seasonal adjustment technique will be incorporated in the report on the study.

GEORGE R. MORRISON

BANKING MARKETS AND BANK STRUCTURE

An exploratory study is being undertaken, with the aid of a grant from the American Bankers Association, to develop plans for research in banking structure, markets, and performance. Among the topics to be considered will be the effects of bank structure on the pricing of banking services, on cost behavior, on competition, and on the availability of credit to local areas.

The immediate objective of this endeavor is the formulation of one or more specific research proposals, if the exploration suggests their desirability and feasibility. Such projects would involve an analysis of the influence of differential banking structure and regulatory policies upon the performance of banks in the economy, but they would be focused on the development of essential facts and relationships, not on the formulation of policy proposals.

As part of the exploratory program, an advisory committee has been appointed to suggest research topics and to review proposals developed by the staff. The members are Lester V. Chandler, Princeton University (*chairman*); David A. Alhadeff, University of California; John J. Balles, Mellon National Bank and Trust Company; Milton Friedman, National Bureau of Economic Research; Raymond E. Hengren, Federal Deposit Insurance Corporation; Donald R. Hodgman, University of Illinois; Robert C. Holland, Board of Governors of the Federal Reserve System; Clifton H. Kreps, Jr., University of North Carolina; Wesley Lindow, Irving Trust Company; Thomas G. Moore, Carnegie Institute of Technology; Roger F. Murray, National Bureau of Economic Research; Almarin Phillips, University of Pennsylvania; Roland I. Robinson, Michigan State University; Marvin E. Rozen, Pennsylvania State University; Edward S. Shaw, Stanford University; Robert P. Shay, National Bureau of Economic Research; Charls E. Walker, American Bankers Association.

DONALD P. JACOBS
GEORGE R. MORRISON

CONSUMER CREDIT

The general objective of this study is to assess the role of consumer credit in the economy of the United States. Attention is centered on analysis of consumer behavior, the level and structure of finance rates and costs, and the functioning of credit markets as affected by economic and legislative forces. The study is supported by general grants from several finance companies.

Five publications have resulted from the study to date, and several more are expected in the near future. Already published are:

> *Cost of Providing Consumer Credit: A Study of Four Major Types of Financial Institutions,* by Paul F. Smith (Occasional Paper 83)
>
> *Trends and Cycles in the Commercial Paper Market,* by Richard T. Selden (Occasional Paper 85)
>
> *New-Automobile Finance Rates, 1924-62,* by Robert P. Shay (Occasional Paper 86)
>
> *Consumer Sensitivity to Finance Rates: An Empirical and Analytical Investigation,* by F. Thomas Juster and Robert P. Shay (Occasional Paper 88)

Consumer Credit Costs, 1949-59, by Paul F. Smith (Studies in Consumer Instalment Financing 11)

An Occasional Paper by Philip A. Klein, *Financial Adjustments to Unemployment,* is in press. The monograph by Wallace P. Mors, "Consumer Credit Finance Charges: Rate Information and Quotation," will go to the printer soon.

In addition to the studies in progress, described below, a summary report on the entire study is planned.

Robert P. Shay

Consumer Finances

A manuscript with the tentative title "Trends in Consumer Investment and Consumer Credit, 1897-1962" has been circulated to a staff reading committee. The first section of the report is a conceptual and empirical analysis of trends in gross fixed capital formation, using alternative definitions of capital formation. It is argued that an appropriately broad definition of capital formation yields estimates with a markedly different long-term trend than the narrower definitions that have been more traditional. Treating outlays on major consumer durable goods and government structures as capital formation leads to the conclusion that gross fixed capital formation has persistently risen relative to gross national product. If, in addition, outlays on certain types of services (education plus research and development) are also treated as capital formation, the rise has been even more rapid in recent decades.

The second section compares the cyclical variability of household fixed investment with that of investment by business enterprises. The data indicate that the absolute variability of household investment became considerably larger than that of business investment during the period after 1945, while the reverse had been true in earlier periods. The third section contrasts the degree to which the household and business enterprise sectors borrow funds in the capital market in order to finance investment outlays. Again, in the early decades after the turn of the century, household borrowing was relatively unimportant compared to business borrowing, but during the postwar period the two sectors drew on capital markets to roughly the same extent. Probably at least some part of the very rapid growth of household borrowing must be attributed to a secular decline in the cost of borrowing. Not only have mortgage and instalment finance rates declined but, more importantly, the maturities available on all types of consumer credit contracts have shown a marked tendency to lengthen. The latter phenomenon can be viewed as a decline in effective borrowing costs.

A considerable amount of work—both data compilation and equation fitting—has been done on the relation between credit terms and outlays for consumer durables, which had originally been planned as part of the above-mentioned manuscript. Difficulties in interpreting the results—caused in part by the question of which price index for certain durables (autos and housing, mainly) is most accurate—has slowed the progress of this research. Some interesting results have been obtained, and I am now testing the results of alternative stock and flow demand equations that use official price indexes as well as some newer ones that make explicit allowance for the alleged underestimate of quality change in the official indexes.

One incidental outcome of this research is the finding that many studies of the price elasticity of demand for durables make use of price indexes that are conceptually inconsistent with the quantity series used. Another incidental but interesting finding is that immense variation exists in estimates of price change for some durables—notably automobiles. For example, the official price indexes show that automobile prices rose by roughly 150 per cent between 1929 and 1962. Reasonable quality-adjusted price indexes can be constructed that show a rise of only 30 per cent over the same span.

F. Thomas Juster

RATE STRUCTURE IN
AUTOMOBILE FINANCING

Revisions of the annual new-auto finance rate series published in *New-Auto Finance Rates, 1924-62* (Occasional Paper 86) have been carried out to obtain consistency between quarterly estimates and the annual series, correct a posting error affecting the 1954-55 base-year period, and extend the series back from 1924 to 1919. Table IV-11 compares the revised series with the series published in the Occasional Paper.

Research during the past year has been devoted to analysis of the extensive regression computations undertaken in earlier years. Further research was undertaken to strengthen the analysis of 1954-55 direct bank loan contracts when it became apparent that a large proportion of the explained variation had been captured inadvertently by state legal-ceiling variables which did not show expected relations to height of the ceiling. Consequently other state variables, such as the legal status of branch banking and number of banks, were substituted successfully in place of the legal-ceiling variables. In comparison with unit-banking states, unlimited branch banking was associated with lower rates; but among those states with unlimited branch banking, states with larger numbers of branches per 1,000 population charged significantly higher rates. Finance rates in states with limited branch banking did not prove significantly lower than in unit-banking states, nor was the corresponding relation for the number of branches significantly higher. The size of metropolitan area was consistently associated with rates of charge, with lower rates especially noticeable in metropolitan areas composed of 500,000 or more population.

The remaining work to be completed involves improvement of the mathematical model used in empirical investigation of the demand for new automobiles between 1929 and 1962, analysis of finance rates in used-car financing, and consideration of the division of the finance rates between automobile dealers and sales finance companies in both new- and used-car financing. One basic obstacle hampering the time series analysis of the demand for new automobiles is the lack of satisfactory price indexes which can be used to investigate relative price changes as a factor affecting unit sales. The problem is discussed more fully in Juster's report, above.

ROBERT P. SHAY

FINANCE RATE CEILINGS

The effects of legal ceilings upon finance rates in new- and used-automobile financing is the subject of this proposed Occasional Paper. Chapters dealing with new-auto financing in 1954-55 and 1958-59 are ready for internal staff review. The remaining chapter analyzes used-car financing and will be ready for staff review shortly.

WALLACE P. MORS

THE QUALITY OF CREDIT IN BOOMS AND DEPRESSIONS

I have now completed a draft of what is presently planned as a small book, "The Quality of Postwar Credit in the United States." It summarizes the highlights of the several quality-of-credit studies that have been supported in large part by a grant from the Merrill Foundation for the Advancement of Financial Knowledge. The manuscript is being revised, and I hope it will be ready for staff review this summer. Its chapter titles are as follows:

    I. Introduction
   II. The Changing Weight of Postwar Debt
  III. Credit Characteristics and Performance
  IV. Credit Quality and Postwar Business Cycles
   V. The Postwar Trend in Quality Characteristics
  VI. The Postwar Performance Record
 VII. Some Tentative Conclusions

TABLE IV-11

New-Auto Finance Rate Annual Estimates, 1919-64, Four Large Sales Finance Companies

Year	Average Finance Rate (per cent) Old Series	Average Finance Rate (per cent) Revised Series	NBER Index (1954-55=100) Old Series	NBER Index (1954-55=100) Revised Series
1919	n.a.	13.99	n.a.	123
1920	n.a.	13.51	n.a.	119
1921	n.a.	14.36	n.a.	126
1922	n.a.	13.75	n.a.	121
1923	n.a.	15.09	n.a.	132
1924	15.23	15.33	135	135
1925	14.09	14.19	125	125
1926	14.09	14.19	125	125
1927	15.09	15.19	133	133
1928	15.23	15.33	135	135
1929	15.23	15.33	135	135
1930	15.23	15.33	135	135
1931	14.95	15.05	132	132
1932	16.94	17.05	150	150
1933	16.94	17.05	150	150
1934	16.51	16.62	146	146
1935	14.40	14.40	127	126
1936	11.74	11.74	104	103
1937	11.74	11.74	104	103
1938	11.63	11.63	103	102
1939	11.63	11.63	103	102
1940	11.63	11.63	103	102
1941	11.63	11.63	103	102
1946	11.20	11.28	99	99
1947	11.20	11.28	99	99
1948	11.98	12.07	106	106
1949	11.76	11.84	104	104
1950	11.09	11.16	98	98
1951	10.98	11.05	97	97
1952	11.09	11.16	98	98
1953	11.20	11.28	99	99
1954	11.20	11.35	99	100
1955	11.42	11.41	101	100
1956	11.90	11.90	105	104
1957	12.35	12.35	109	108
1958	12.36	12.39	109	109
1959	12.41	12.43	110	109
1960	12.46	12.47	110	109
1961	12.44	12.45	110	109
1962	12.15	12.16	107	107
1963	n.a.	11.76	n.a.	103
1964	n.a.	11.34	n.a.	100

Notes to Table IV-11

SOURCE: Same as Table 8, page 21, *New-Auto Finance Rates,* with the following additions and corrections:

1919-24: Representative transactions were obtained from records of one large sales finance company, and estimates of finance rates for each year were calculated. An index of this company's rates in terms of its 1936-38 base-period average rate was linked to the four-company NBER index (1954-55=100) by multiplying each year of the single-company index by the ratio of the 1924 value of the NBER index to the 1924 value of the single-company index. The product was multiplied by the 1954-55 base-period four-company average finance rate (11.39 per cent) to obtain the four-company finance rate estimates.

1924-41: The 1936-38 average rate (11.703 per cent) was 0.81667 of the base-period (1924-41=100) index average. So, solving 11.703=0.81667x, the 1924-41 average for the period was 14.330, and estimates of finance rates were computed by multiplying this figure by the Haberler index (*Consumer Instalment Credit and Economic Fluctuations,* New York, NBER, 1942, p. 91) as adjusted for each year.

1946-55: The 1954-55 average rate (11.39 per cent) was equivalent to the Federal Reserve index average of 101 (1946=100), and rates in other years were computed by multiplying 11.39 per cent by $x/101$, where x is any given value of the Federal Reserve index.

Plans for a summary statistical volume bringing together the various monthly, quarterly, and annual series on credit quality that have been used or developed in our investigations have been drawn up. The volume will include historical data pertaining to both the terms on which credit has been extended and the financial status of the borrowers, together with descriptions of the sources and nature of the statistics and a guide to their interpretation. Edgar Fiedler will take charge of this work, beginning this spring, and the Bankers Trust Company has offered to bear a substantial share of the costs.

Two reports in this program of studies have been published: *The Quality of Bank Loans: A Study of Bank Examination Records,* by Albert M. Wojnilower (Occasional Paper 82); and *The Quality of Trade Credit,* by Martin H. Seiden (Occasional Paper 87). The status of the remaining studies on individual credit sectors follows:

1. The manuscript by Geoffrey Moore and Philip Klein on consumer instalment credit quality is almost completed in its revised form.

2. Thomas Atkinson is revising and extending his manuscript of an Occasional Paper, "Postwar Corporate Bond Quality," following staff review.

3. George Brinegar and Lyle P. Fettig have submitted manuscripts dealing with the quality of Federal Land Bank farm mortgages and Production Credit Administration short-term loans to farmers. It is hoped that these two manuscripts can be summarized in an Occasional Paper for early publication.

4. A brief report on the current study of the factors affecting residential mortgage delinquency and foreclosure appears below.

JAMES S. EARLEY

The Quality of Mortgage Credit

Much of the past year has been spent in gathering and putting into comparable form data received from the United States Savings and Loan League, the Mortgage Bankers Association, and the National Association of Mutual Savings Banks' delinquency surveys. With the receipt of the NAMSB figures in November, the data-gathering phase of the project was completed. Some minor difficulties remain, however, in getting the information in such a form that it can be handled as pooled data by our electronic data processing systems.

The analytical phase of the work has been largely devoted to preliminary analyses of the data we have had on hand, in order to determine what statistical models are likely to work best, given the nature of the data. As a result of these studies, we plan to employ multiple regression techniques, chi-square analysis, and possibly multiple discriminant analysis to derive and test various "indexes" of mortgage quality. We plan this summer to finish a draft of an Occasional Paper incorporating these results, together with other material relating to postwar residential mortgage quality.

The study has been supported by grants from the above-mentioned organizations as well as by other funds of the National Bureau.

JAMES S. EARLEY
JOHN P. HERZOG

INCOME FROM EMPLOYMENT UNDER THE PERSONAL INCOME TAX

Extensive revisions in this manuscript, which was reviewed by a staff reading committee in 1963, have been made and the text will shortly be ready for review by the Directors.

The study is essentially in three parts: (1) the coverage of employment income on tax returns, (2) the pattern of income reported on the returns with wages and salaries, and (3) the tax liability attributable to employment income and how specific provisions applicable to wages and salaries have affected this share in tax liability. Most of the revisions made in the past year were concentrated in the last part, which is also the most extensive of the three.

I find that the impact on tax liability of specific provisions applicable largely, or entirely, to income from employment has not been very large, on the average. The mean effective rate of income tax on estimated total wages and salaries (adjusted to conform to income tax definitions) for 1960 was 11.1 per cent. If the income tax concept of wages and salaries is expanded so as to encompass all forms of employee compensation, such as employer contributions to retirement systems, payments in kind ordinarily not construed as taxable, sick pay and employer-financed medical care insurance, and so on, the mean effective rate drops to 10.4 per cent. As part of the revisions of the past year, the mean effective tax rate on total property income—also defined to include both realized and unrealized amounts—was computed in addition to that on total employee compensation. Both sets of effective rates were estimated by income groups to eliminate the influence on over-all effective rates of differences in the income size distribution of employee compensation and property income.

C. HARRY KAHN

OTHER STUDIES

The following reports were published: *Research in the Capital Markets,* National Bureau Exploratory Committee on Research in the Capital Markets; *The Flow of Capital Funds in the Postwar Economy,* Raymond W. Goldsmith; *The Measurement of Corporate Sources and Uses of Funds,* David Meiselman and Eli Shapiro; *The Quality of Trade Credit,* Martin H. Seiden; and *Determinants and Effects of Changes in the Stock of Money, 1875-1960,* by Phillip Cagan.

Lawrence H. Seltzer is revising his study, "The Personal Exemptions in the Federal Income Tax," for submission to the Board.

Other studies of financial institutions and processes are reported by Ture and others in section 1; by Murray, Holland, Dickinson, and Nelson in section 2; by Friedman and Schwartz and by Lipsey and Preston in section 3.

5. INTERNATIONAL ECONOMIC RELATIONS

EXPORTS OF MANUFACTURES BY LESS DEVELOPED COUNTRIES

As part of a study of exports of manufactures by less developed countries, I am seeking to identify the products in which these countries might be expected to hold or to gain a competitive advantage. If this information can be developed on the basis of objective criteria, it would be useful both as a check list for appraising the present status of the trade and as a guide to possible future trends.

By definition, the less developed countries have little accumulated capital. Any competitive advantage which they may have in manufacturing, apart from resource-based industries, must come largely from their low wages. Such an advantage is likely to be found in industries with a strong labor orientation—defined here as industries which, compared with other industries, employ labor possessing easily acquired skills and use little machinery and other capital. These two characteristics come to much the same thing: low capital requirements per worker whether in the form of education and training (i.e., human capital) or in the more tangible form of plant and equipment.[1]

A basis for the ranking of industries according to their requirements of both types of capital is readily available for the United States and many foreign countries in the form of value added by manufacture per employee. This measure has the advantage of giving the relevant data in a single series which can be broken down into (1) average wage and salary per employee as an index of input of human capital and (2) average nonwage value added per employee as an index of input of physical

[1] It is assumed, as seems reasonable, that the technological gap between less developed and developed countries would not be greater, and might well be less, in labor-oriented industries than in more capital-intensive industries.

CHART IV-2

Value Added per Employee in U.S. Manufacturing Industry,
by Major (2-Digit SIC) Industry Groups, 1962

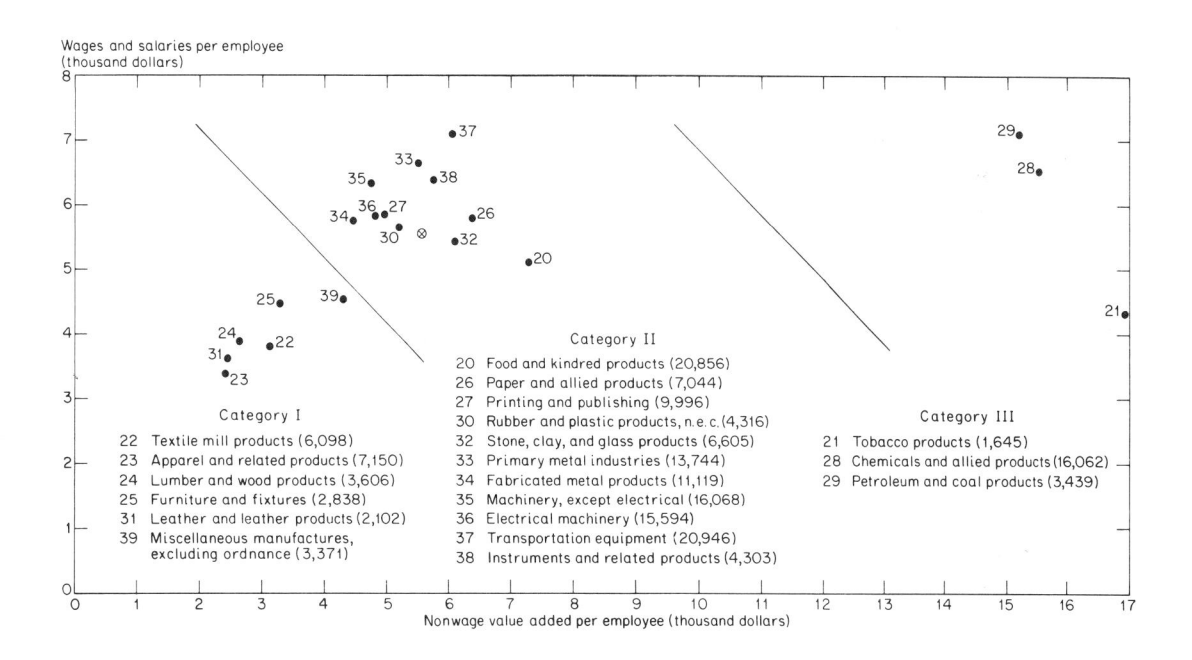

Category I
22 Textile mill products (6,098)
23 Apparel and related products (7,150)
24 Lumber and wood products (3,606)
25 Furniture and fixtures (2,838)
31 Leather and leather products (2,102)
39 Miscellaneous manufactures, excluding ordnance (3,371)

Category II
20 Food and kindred products (20,856)
26 Paper and allied products (7,044)
27 Printing and publishing (9,996)
30 Rubber and plastic products, n.e.c. (4,316)
32 Stone, clay, and glass products (6,605)
33 Primary metal industries (13,744)
34 Fabricated metal products (11,119)
35 Machinery, except electrical (16,068)
36 Electrical machinery (15,594)
37 Transportation equipment (20,946)
38 Instruments and related products (4,303)

Category III
21 Tobacco products (1,645)
28 Chemicals and allied products (16,062)
29 Petroleum and coal products (3,439)

SOURCE: *1962 Annual Survey of Manufactures*, U.S. Bureau of the Census.
⊕Average for all manufacturing industries.

NOTE: Figures in parentheses after industry groups show value added in millions of dollars.

capital.[2]

In Chart IV-2 the twenty major industry groups are plotted according to these measures as derived from the U.S. *Survey of Manufactures* for 1962. The points seem to fall into three distinct groups. Six are clustered in the lower left-hand area of the chart designated as Category I. They average only $6,700 in value added per employee, including a wage component of $3,800 and a nonwage component of $2,900. These low figures suggest a strong labor orientation.

The eleven major industry groups in Category II have an average value added per employee of $11,600. All of them are higher than the highest in Category I in both wage and nonwage value added, and, on these criteria, require much more human and physical capital per worker.

The three industry groups in Category III in the chart yield the high average of $22,000 for value added per employee and are all very close to this average. They are not above the range of the industry groups in Category II in average wage (and one, tobacco, is in fact below that range), but they are very distant indeed in nonwage value added, which alone averages $15,600 per employee. This figure doubtless reflects the high capital investment (including inventories in the case of tobacco) required to manipulate and process the materials used in these industries. Differences in the cost of labor seem likely to play less of a role in the location of these industries than differences in the cost and availability of capital. But the latter in turn depends heavily in many cases on where the raw materials are found, on the costs of exploiting them and of transporting them in crude or refined state, and on other conditions determining access to markets. It seems justified therefore to regard industries in Category III as largely resource-oriented.

The individual industries composing the groups in Category I are relatively homogeneous with respect to both wage and nonwage value added. Very few of them fall beyond the range indicated for the category.[3] Some of the interesting exceptions of a more capital-intensive nature are knit fabrics and tufted carpets in the textile group, prefabricated products in the lumber and wood products group, and metal office furniture in the furniture and fixtures group. The industries making up the groups in Category III are also very homogeneous, though a few items, including agricultural chemicals and paints and varnishes, are in the range given for Category II, and one, cigars, falls into Category I.

Category II is not only much larger than the other two in total value added but also much more heterogeneous in composition. A few of the components which, in a more detailed breakdown, fall in Category I (and which, by their names, suggest a relatively strong labor orientation) are greeting cards, rubber footwear, tiles, pottery, office computing machines, electronic components, and motorcycles and bicycles. An important and strongly resource-oriented industry which moves up to Category III is primary nonferrous metals out of the primary metals group.

Until a few years ago, it had come to be generally accepted in economic theory that a grouping of industries by factor intensities based on observations for one country, such as that given in Chart IV-2, would probably be generally valid for other countries as well, even for those with a quite different relation

---

[2] Differences in average wage and salary per employee are here taken as measuring differences between industries in the quality of labor employed (including not only "production workers" but also managers, engineers, scientists, and other salaried personnel) and not as measuring interindustry differences in the cost of labor of a given quality. No attempt is made in this note to examine the rationale of this and other assumptions involved in the present approach. Among the questions requiring further study is how industries rank in capital intensity by the method followed here compared with other measures.

[3] The 45-degree lines marking the boundaries between the categories connect points of equal value added per employee (sum of the wage and nonwage ordinates) and are drawn midway between the overall averages of the categories on either side.

between wage costs and capital costs.[4] To be sure, countries with plentiful manpower and low wage rates would tend to employ more labor in relation to capital than other countries. But this would be a general phenomenon characterizing the whole range of industry without significantly altering from one country to another the ranking of industries in terms of their relative factor intensities. These were thought to be determined mainly by the technical conditions of production, so that, for instance, the capital per worker required in steel compared with that in textiles need not vary appreciably with differences in relative wage and capital costs.

Except to the extent that some of them might be favored with resource-oriented industries, poor countries with abundant manpower and little capital would therefore tend to specialize in labor-oriented industries of the type here placed in Category I, while more highly developed countries would specialize in industries requiring more equipment and more highly qualified manpower. How far this specialization proceeded and how much effect it had in equalizing returns to labor and capital internationally would depend on the extent of obstacles to trade, including transport costs, tariffs, quantitative restrictions, and hidden barriers. It would also depend on any special obstacles within countries impeding the development of industry in accordance with comparative advantages.

Recent research has produced arguments and some empirical results at variance with the view just summarized and has given prominence to possibilities previously regarded as interesting but probably minor exceptions to the rule.[5] This newer approach, if sound, would have among its consequences that one could not confidently rank industries according to their relative requirements of labor, capital, and other factors of production, nor look at the relative factor endowments of different countries for clues to the likely composition and development of international trade.

In view of their potentially important implications for expectations and policies concerning international trade and economic development, these conflicting views need to be carefully examined. Chart IV-3 presents some relevant data drawn from a recent United Nations publication giving summary statistics for a number of countries according to the International Standard Industrial Classification (in which, it must be noted, code numbers and industry group definitions differ from those of the United States Standard Industrial Classification used in Chart IV-2). Unfortunately, comparable and adequate data are lacking for many countries which one would like to include, notable examples being France and Italy among the industrially developed countries. The group of less developed countries shown in the chart consists of only eight, in which India alone has a weight of almost 50 per cent. Another disadvantage for present purposes is that the national data have been condensed into only thirteen industry groups of widely differing size and homogeneity. Comparisons between countries, especially between developed and less developed countries, are likely to be thrown off by differences in the products and product mix of what is ostensibly the same industry group.[6]

---

[4] For a fuller statement of this view and of the criticisms of it discussed below, see Michael Michaely, "Factor Proportions in International Trade: Current State of the Theory," *Kyklos,* Vol. 17, 1964.

[5] See particularly Bagicha Singh Minhas, *An International Comparison of Factor Costs and Factor Use,* Amsterdam, 1963.

[6] The rubber products industry (group 30 of the ISIC) illustrates the problem. In the United States in 1962, value added per employee was $14,810 in tires and tubes compared with $7,900 in rubber footwear and $10,330 in other rubber manufactures. The extraordinarily high rank of this industry in the less developed country series (heavily influenced in this respect by India) may therefore reflect the success which a number of these countries have had in inducing the large American and European tire manufacturers to establish plants in their areas.

Another noticeable deviation from the U.S. pattern is the high average value added in basic metals (34 of the ISIC) in several of the foreign series. In Japan this result stems mainly from relatively high wages and salaries in this industry in relation to the average level in that country. In the other industrial

CHART IV-3

Comparative Structure of Manufacturing in the United States and Selected Foreign Countries with Respect to Value Added (Wage and Nonwage) per Employee in Thirteen Industry Groups (ISIC), 1958
(average for all manufacturing industry in each country or country group = 100)[a]

SOURCE: Computed from country tables in *The Growth of World Industry,* United Nations, 1963.

NOTE: *Industry Groups:* The industry groups specified in the chart are from the International Standard Industrial Classification as consolidated in the UN source noted below. The sequence in each panel is the ascending order for the United States.

20-22. Food, beverages, and tobacco
23. Textiles
24. Clothing, footwear, and made-up textiles
25-26. Wood products and furniture
27. Paper and paper products
28. Printing and publishing
29. Leather and leather and fur products
30. Rubber products
31-32. Chemicals and chemical, petroleum, and coal products
33. Nonmetallic mineral products
34. Basic metals
35-38. Metal products
39. Other manufacturing

[a] The indexes for the two country groups are obtained by combining the national indexes weighted according to total employment in manufacturing in each country. The composition of the country groups and the weights assigned to each member are as follows:

Seven industrial countries: Australia (8.9), Canada (11.3), Denmark (2.8), Germany (57.6), Netherlands (9.8), Norway (2.5), Sweden (7.1).

Eight less developed countries: Argentina (15.9), Brazil (21.4), Chile (2.9), Colombia (3.1), India (48.3), Pakistan (5.5), Peru (1.6), and Venezuela (1.3).

In a few exceptional and minor cases, the index number for a particular industry is based on less than the full number of countries listed for the group.

Under these circumstances, the similarity of the industrial profiles for different countries or country groups in Chart IV-3 is impressive. The comparison of value added per employee in panel A is the most pertinent, since the division between the wage and nonwage components may vary from country to country or, within countries, from industry to industry for both institutional and statistical reasons. Even so, in all three series relatively high coefficients of rank correlation (Spearman) are obtained between the data for the United States and those for other countries, to wit:

Value Added per Employee

Correlation Between the United States and	Total	Wages and Salaries	Other
United Kingdom	.912	.874	.907
Japan	.835	.907	.742
Seven other industrial countries	.978	.956	.918
Eight less developed countries	.901	.725	.791

Scrutiny of the chart shows, moreover, that the principal deviations in the patterns concern industries in the middle and upper ranges of the value added scale. If one focuses on the five industry groups on the left side of panel A, it will be seen that they all rank below other industry groups in each of the foreign series, as they do in that for the United States. And these are the industries which correspond, *grosso modo,* to those in Category I of Chart IV-2; i.e., apparel, textiles, wood products and furniture, leather and leather products, and miscellaneous manufactures.

An analysis of the type briefly sketched above is intended to serve as the point of departure for a systematic examination of the actual development of exports of manufactures by less developed countries to the United States and Western Europe. Particular attention will be given to differences in the results for different products and for different exporting and importing countries. It is hoped that the study will also throw light on the nature of the obstacles, on either side, to the development of this trade and will help to indicate its potentialities.

HAL B. LARY

UNITED STATES PERFORMANCE IN INTERNATIONAL TRADE

The collection of the data required for this project, which has been supported by a National Science Foundation grant, has been completed, and drafting of the manuscript reporting on the findings has begun. It is divided into three parts. Part I deals with changes in the composition of U.S. exports. Part II deals with an analysis of interindustrial country trade; more specifically, it analyzes changes in the imports of each industrial country from every other industrial country. In Part III an attempt is made to establish relations between foreign trade and domestic variables for each industrial country with a view to providing explanatory hypotheses for the changes in trade found in the other parts. The period covered is 1953-55 to 1960-62.

H. G. GEORGIADIS

INTERNATIONAL PRICE COMPARISON STUDY

This project attempts to develop methods for evaluating the price competitiveness of an industrial economy in world trade and to apply these methods to measuring the competitive position of the United States in machinery, vehicles, and other metal products since 1953. The study has been financed by two grants from the National Science Foundation.

Data for price measurements are being collected from over 150 American firms that buy

---

country group and the less developed country group, however, the difference in rank arises mainly in nonwage value added and may reflect a high share of nonferrous metal production compared with steel production, value added per employee being substantially higher in the first than in the second (according to details for the United States).

or sell these products in international markets, from U.S. government agencies which receive bids by both domestic and foreign suppliers, and from sources in foreign countries, both governmental and private. Two sets of data collected from foreign sources have now been turned in and a third is nearing completion. There is a possibility that one or two additional foreign price collections will be undertaken. Some further data gathering from both government and private sources will still be required to bring the measurement of price relationships down to 1964 and to fill gaps revealed in the course of the analysis.

A discussion of the study's aims and methods, with preliminary data on iron and steel products, is in press as an Occasional Paper. A summary of this paper was presented at a joint meeting of the American Economic Association and the American Statistical Association in December 1964. Some of the tentative findings on iron and steel are shown in Table IV-12.

Price indexes for internationally traded iron and steel products, composed of export prices for products exported by each country and domestic prices for other products, are shown in the first section of the table under the heading "international price indexes." Prices of the U.S., the U.K., and the EEC countries moved in the same direction in all but one of the periods shown. They all rose in 1953-57 and 1963-64, and fell between 1961 and 1962. The exception was 1957-61, when U.K. and EEC prices fell substantially from their Suez-crisis levels, while U.S. prices were comparatively stable.

European price levels for iron and steel products, shown in the second part of the table, were lower than U.S. prices in every year listed. The gap was greatest, at about 20 per cent, in 1962 and 1963, and then, according to very preliminary estimates, narrowed to about 15 per cent in 1964. The U.S. position was more favorable in 1953 and 1957, when European prices were about 10 per cent below those of the United States.

Since international price relations are often inferred from domestic price data, we have made some computations on that basis for comparison. Conclusions from these prices could be quite different from those drawn from the NBER international price indexes. The domestic price indexes indicate a much smaller decline in European prices between 1957 and 1963, and no rise from 1963 to 1964, when the NBER indexes point to an increase of 12 to 13 per cent. Judging by the domestic price indexes, therefore, one would find much less of a relative increase in U.S. prices between 1957 and 1962. From 1963 to 1964, the domestic prices suggest a further deterioration in the competitive position of the United States (as measured by price movements), and the NBER international price series suggest a turn toward improvement.

During 1965 this study will be concerned mainly with analysis of the large volume of data we have now collected, with greater emphasis on the study of the machinery and vehicles areas, and then the preparation of a report on the project as a whole. Elizabeth Durbin, who has been responsible for much of the data collection from American companies, will now shift to the collating and summarizing of this material with the help of Jocelyn Coburn, who joined the study in the summer.

IRVING B. KRAVIS
ROBERT E. LIPSEY
PHILIP J. BOURQUE

FOREIGN TRADE AND BUSINESS CYCLES

Instability of earnings from exports has long been of concern to policy makers; yet the sources and nature of this instability are only vaguely perceived, and proposals for stabilization thus rest on shaky foundations and are highly controversial. Is it true, for instance, as often claimed, that the main trouble is with primary exports, while exports of industrial products are fairly stable? Or that the gyrations of primary export receipts are to be attributed to prices rather than volumes? Several interesting investigations bearing on these

TABLE IV-12

Indexes of International Prices, Iron and Steel, SITC Division 67

	1953	1957	1961	1962	1963	1964
International Price Indexes (1962 = 100)						
U.S.	86	100	101	100	98	103
U.K.	96	108	103	100	98	109
EEC	96	117	105	100	98	110
International Price Levels (U.S. = 100)						
U.S.	100	100	100	100	100	100
U.K.	94	91	84	81	81	85
EEC	89	92	82	80	79	85

NOTE: The International price indexes are derived solely from time-to-time price relatives. These are aggregated from four-digit and, occasionally, five-digit SITC classifications, using world trade weights.

The 1962 international price levels are aggregates of place-to-place price comparisons. For other years the price levels were not derived by aggregating place-to-place data but were, instead, calculated from our "indexes of price competitiveness." These can be derived either by dividing the time-to-time index for the U.S. by the corresponding U.K. index, for example, or by dividing the ratio of U.K. to U.S. price levels for one year by the ratio for another year. Since the indexes of price competitiveness measure changes in the place-to-place ratios, they imply, given one year's ratio as a starting point, place-to-place indexes for the other years. The indexes of price competitiveness used for this computation were calculated from a mixture of place-to-place and time-to-time data, and therefore do not precisely match the international price indexes shown.

questions have been published lately, but the empirical evidence they provide is still tentative and partly contradictory.

The last chapter of my own study of cycles in U.S. exports reveals certain new facts on export instability which agree with common notions but disagree in other important respects. It presents measures of the instability of quantity, price, and value series for the four major commodity classes of U.S. exports (finished manufactures, semimanufactures, crude materials, and foods). The measures cover two periods: 1879-1913 and 1921-61. But curiously, the instability of exports is so persistent over time that most of its features hold for the entire period covered.

The most widely accepted view of the nature of these relations seems to be that fluctuations in export proceeds of primary producers are largely fluctuations in prices, while exports of manufactures are characterized by rigid prices and large swings in quantities. Furthermore, quantity and price of all export classes are thought to move in the same direction, and values hence to fluctuate more than quantities. My findings agree with these expectations in some respects. For instance, the behavior of exports of manufactures is as expected in the sense that quantity changes far more than price, and that both move together so that value is more unstable than quantity. That prices of primary goods (crude materials and foods) have wider swings than prices of manufactures is also confirmed. But the agreement ends when we turn to the measures of instability of the quantities of semimanufactures, crude materials, and foods exported from the U.S. We find that quantities of all classes are a great deal more variable than the corresponding prices. (The average annual rates of change of the former are two to three times as high as those of the latter.)

Further, the quantities and values of nonmanufactures are not less but far more volatile than those of manufactures, though the latter also are far from stable. But the movements in manufactures of 10 to 15 per cent a year on the average do not match the 19 to 36 per cent a year variations in the remaining classes.[7] That semimanufactures moved nearly twice as much as finished manufactures but still not as much as crude materials argues for the internal consistency of these measures.

We are thus faced with the question: Why do our findings and those of some others conflict with plausible views on export instability and with evidence supporting such views? Why are the swings in export quantities far larger than those in prices in all commodity classes, according to our measures, and why do manufactures quantities fluctuate less, not more, than those of other classes?

The answer is partly that the contrary views and the evidence on which they are based are drawn from the extraordinary cycles caused by the world wars and the great depression, but do not hold for normal short business cycles. Major cycles, when included, dominate the picture, and this is even more true where the role of mild swings is reduced by the use of annual data. The opposite holds for our measures from which the extraordinary cycles are excluded.

That the behavior of exports differs between normal and unusual business cycles is plausible for two reasons. First, supply responds relatively more strongly to mild changes in foreign demand than to enormous ones. Second, shifts in supply play a greater role in normal than in extraordinary cycles. As regards the first point, it is true that supply of primary goods cannot expand in proportion to tremendous war demands or plunge as deeply as demand did in the 1930's. The fact that these demand changes were expected to be transitory may also have contributed to the unresponsiveness of supply. But this does not mean that normal fluctuations in foreign demand for primary goods cannot encounter sufficient supply elasticity for large variations in export quantities to occur. Stocks can be built up or drawn down, and domestic consumption of export goods can be expanded or contracted. The last point plays a particularly large role in the United States, but would not hold for countries which do not consume their own export goods.

This explanation derives further support from another set of our measures: when we isolate that part of the total cyclical movement which can be regarded as determined by foreign demand, we again find that quantities fluctuate more than prices in U.S. exports of crude materials and foods.

A second factor to which differences among findings may be attributed is the effect of the degree of aggregation on the degree of instability. Quantities of different export commodities are likely to reach their peaks and troughs at different times, which reduces the amplitudes of swings in large-quantity aggregates. The timing of price movements, on the other hand, shows less diversity, and thus their amplitudes are less affected by aggregation. Hence, studies of world trade find the quantity of primary exports more stable relative to price than studies of individual countries or individual commodities, and the prevailing view may hold for total world exports but not for exports of most individual countries.

ILSE MINTZ

OTHER STUDIES

Herbert B. Woolley's manuscript "Measuring Transactions Between World Areas" is now in press.

Walther P. Michael has completed a revision of his manuscript "International Capital Movements, 1950-54."

A new study of balance-of-payments adjustments in various countries in the postwar period, to be undertaken by Michael Michaely, is described in Part III.

---

[7] Measured by expressing the annual change from trough to peak to trough in the quarterly series as a percentage of its average level during the same cycle.

Besides the research conducted by its own staff, the National Bureau from time to time arranges special conferences and also sponsors two continuing groups that plan and organize conferences on research. University, government, and other specialists in particular fields participate in these conferences. They are invited to prepare papers growing out of their own research and to discuss those prepared by others. The revised papers are, in most instances, submitted to the National Bureau for publication in conference proceedings volumes. A list of the volumes published last year or in press, together with future scheduled conferences, follows.

PART V

Conferences on Research

CONFERENCE PROCEEDINGS PUBLISHED
SINCE JANUARY 1, 1964

The Behavior of Income Shares: Selected Theoretical and Empirical Issues (Studies in Income and Wealth, Vol. 27, 1964, x + 394 pp., $8.00). Contains papers on theories of income distribution; factor shares in the long term; capital, labor, and income in manufacturing; short-run movements of income shares; long-run changes in income distribution by factor shares in Canada; analysis of factor shares by industry; and estimation of produced income by state and region.

Models of Income Determination (Studies in Income and Wealth, Vol. 28, 1964, ix + 427 pp., $10.00). Contains nine papers presented at a meeting of the Conference on Research in Income and Wealth, together with comments on them. Reports on experiments in the use of national income and related data for constructing either complete models of income determination and forecasting or individual structural relations which can be used in such models.

The Role of Direct and Indirect Taxes in the Federal Revenue System (Conference held under the auspices of the National Bureau of Economic Research and the Brookings Institution, 1964, xii + 321 pp., $7.50; paperbound, $2.95). Examines the differential effects of indirect and direct taxes on personal effort, saving, investment, allocation of resources, and

91

the efficiency of business operations. Considers the increasing federal use of indirect taxes on the distribution of tax burdens, the fiscal position of states and localities, and our balance-of-payments situation. Also investigates the experience of other countries with direct and indirect taxes.

Measuring the Nation's Wealth (Studies in Income and Wealth, Vol. 29, 1964, xxxi + 835 pp., $6.00). This Joint Economic Committee print, which was developed by the Wealth Inventory Planning Study of the George Washington University, has been included in the Studies in Income and Wealth and is being made available by the National Bureau in order that it may receive general distribution. The report represents the most comprehensive review to date of the state of knowledge in an important and relatively underdeveloped area of national accounts, that is, balance-sheet and wealth estimation. It contains recommendations for the expansion of the collection of wealth data by federal statistical agencies as a basis for continuing balance-sheet and wealth estimates to supplement the national income and product accounts.

CONFERENCE PROCEEDINGS IN PRESS

Transportation Economics (Special Conference 17).

Output, Employment, and Productivity in the United States After 1800 (Studies in Income and Wealth 30).

Foreign Tax Policies and Economic Growth (Conference held under the auspices of the National Bureau of Economic Research and the Brookings Institution).

CONFERENCE PROCEEDINGS IN PREPARATION FOR PRESS

"National Economic Planning" (Special Conference 18).

"Measurement and Interpretation of Job Vacancies" (Special Conference).

CONFERENCES BEING ARRANGED

Investment Behavior, Conference of the Universities-National Bureau Committee for Economic Research, June 10-12, 1965.

Production Relations, Conference on Research in Income and Wealth, October 15-16, 1965.

Economics of Defense, Conference of the Universities-National Bureau Committee for Economic Research, April 1966.

Industrial Composition of Income and Product, Conference on Research in Income and Wealth, Autumn, 1966.

CONFERENCE ON RESEARCH IN INCOME AND WEALTH

The Conference on Industrial Composition of Income and Product, originally scheduled for April 1965, has been postponed until autumn 1966.

A Conference on Production Relations, under the chairmanship of Murray Brown, will be held on October 15-16, 1965, in New York City. The program consists of:

I. Review of Post-World War II Studies of Production Relations
    Theoretical Developments
        Robert M. Solow, Massachusetts Institute of Technology
    Empirical Results
        Marc Nerlove, Stanford University
    Empirical Results with Special Reference to Canadian Experience
        Thomas K. Rymes, N. H. Lithwick, and G. Post, Carleton University

II. Recent Approaches to Production Function Analysis
    Measurement of Vintage Effects on Capital-Output Relations at the Plant Level
        Michael Gort and Raford Boddy, State University of New York at Buffalo
    On the Production Function of U.S. Manufacturing
        Zvi Griliches, University of Chicago
    A Generalized Model of Production
        Murray Brown, U.S. Department of Commerce, and Alfred H. Conrad, Harvard University

III. The Use of Production Relations for Forecasting and Policy Purposes
    Forecasts of Capital Requirements by Means of Production Relations

Robert Eisner, Northwestern University
  The Use of Production Relations for Policy Purposes
    Richard R. Nelson, The Rand Corporation

Members of the executive committee of the Conference on Research in Income and Wealth are John W. Kendrick (chairman), Jack Alterman, Daniel H. Brill, Donald J. Daly, Richard A. Easterlin, Robert Eisner, Morris R. Goldman, F. Thomas Juster, Robert J. Lampman, Charles L. Schultze, and Mildred E. Courtney (secretary).

UNIVERSITIES-NATIONAL BUREAU COMMITTEE FOR ECONOMIC RESEARCH

The Conference on Economic Planning was held at Princeton, New Jersey, on November 27 and 28, 1964, with Max F. Millikan as chairman. Other members of the planning committee were Abram Bergson, Everett E. Hagen, and Edward S. Mason. The annual meeting of the Universities-National Bureau Committee for Economic Research was held on November 27, 1964, in conjunction with the conference.

The Conference on Investment Behavior was held on June 10-12, 1965, at the University of Wisconsin, Madison, Wisconsin. Robert Ferber, University of Illinois, was chairman, and Irwin Friend, Dale Jorgenson, Edwin Kuh, and Victor Zarnowitz were members of the planning committee.

The Conference on the Economics of Defense is tentatively scheduled to be held in April 1966, with Roland N. McKean, University of California, Los Angeles, as chairman. Evsey Domar, Alain Enthoven, Jack Hirshleifer, G. Warren Nutter, Jerome Rothenberg, Thomas Schelling, and James Schlesinger are also members of the planning committee.

The next annual meeting of the Universities-National Bureau Committee for Economic Research will be held in conjunction with the Conference on the Economics of Defense.

Thirty-two universities offering graduate work in economics and emphasizing research, together with the National Bureau, are represented on the committee. The participating universities and their present representatives follow:

Buffalo	Daniel Hamberg
California, Berkeley	Sherman J. Maisel
California, Los Angeles	Harold M. Somers
Carnegie Institute of Technology	Kalman J. Cohen
Chicago	H. Gregg Lewis
Columbia	William S. Vickrey
Cornell	Chandler Morse
Duke	Joseph J. Spengler
Harvard	John R. Meyer
Illinois	V Lewis Bassie
Indiana	Louis Shere
Iowa State	Karl A. Fox
Johns Hopkins	Carl F. Christ
Massachusetts Institute of Technology	M. A. Adelman
McGill	Earl F. Beach
Michigan	William Haber
Minnesota	James M. Henderson
New School for Social Research	Hans Neisser
New York	Jules Backman
North Carolina	Henry A. Latané
Northwestern	Richard B. Heflebower
Pennsylvania	Richard A. Easterlin
Princeton	Richard A. Musgrave
Queen's	T. M. Brown
Stanford	Moses Abramovitz
Texas	Stephen L. McDonald
Toronto	D. C. MacGregor
Vanderbilt	Rendigs Fels
Virginia	G. Warren Nutter
Washington	Douglass C. North
Wisconsin	James S. Earley
Yale	Richard Ruggles

Other members of the committee include as members at large Raymond T. Bowman, G. A. Elliott, Martin R. Gainsbrugh, Edgar M. Hoover, Walter S. Salant, Herbert Stein, and George J. Stigler; and Solomon Fabricant, representing the National Bureau of Economic Research.

The members of the executive committee are Rendigs Fels (chairman), Carl F. Christ (vice-chairman), Solomon Fabricant, James M. Henderson, John R. Meyer, Douglass C. North, and Walter S. Salant. Robert P. Shay is secretary.

CONFERENCE ON MEASUREMENT AND INTERPRETATION OF JOB VACANCIES

Plans for obtaining comprehensive information on job vacancies in the United States were discussed at a conference on February 11-13, 1965, at the Carnegie Endowment International Center in New York City. The National Bureau organized the conference with the aid of the Office of Manpower, Automation and Training of the U.S. Department of Labor. Robert Ferber, University of Illinois, headed the planning committee for the conference, which included Gary Becker, National Bureau and Columbia University; Martin Gainsbrugh (Daniel Creamer, alternate), National Industrial Conference Board; Nathaniel Goldfinger (Marvin Friedman, alternate), AFL-CIO; Harold Goldstein, Bureau of Labor Statistics; Norman Medvin, Bureau of Employment Security; Albert Rees, University of Chicago; Arthur M. Ross, University of California at Berkeley; Herbert E. Striner, W. E. Upjohn Institute for Employment Research; and Seymour L. Wolfbein (Joseph S. Zeisel, alternate), Office of Manpower, Automation and Training.

The need for carefully assembled information on job openings, classified by occupational skill, industry, and geographic location, has been increasingly recognized of late. The conference was held in order to spur research effort on this subject, bring together the results of various inquiries for comparison and evaluation, draw upon experience in this field abroad, and promote the development of accurate and comprehensive information.

Arthur F. Burns opened the conference and chaired the first session. He noted that "A major need of our time is for a guideline to aid the government in formulating and carrying out its responsibilities under the Employment Act. When the amount of unemployment is larger than the number of job vacancies at existing wages, then the aggregate demand for labor is clearly insufficient to provide employment for everyone who is able, willing, and seeking to work. On the other hand, when the number of vacant jobs is equal to or larger than the number of the unemployed, there is no deficiency of aggregate demand. A sensible guideline for monetary and fiscal policy is, therefore, not the volume or rate of unemployment as such, but rather the relation between the number of the unemployed and the number of job vacancies."

A volume containing the following papers, together with comments on them, is in preparation:

I. Measuring the Current Demand for Labor: Needs for Data

Opening Remarks, Arthur F. Burns, National Bureau of Economic Research

Job Vacancy Measures and Economic Analysis, John T. Dunlop, Harvard University

The Role of Job Vacancy Data for an Active Manpower Policy, Louis Levine, U.S. Employment Service

The Concept of Vacancies in a Dynamic Theory of the Labor Market, Charles C. Holt and Martin H. David, University of Wisconsin

II. Collection and Uses of Job Vacancy Data in Countries Other Than the United States

Foreign Job Vacancy Statistics Programs, William C. Shelton and Arthur F. Neef, U.S. Bureau of Labor Statistics

Collection and Uses of Job Vacancy Data in Canada, W. Thomson, National Employment Service of Canada

Job Vacancies and Structural Change in Japanese Labor Markets, Gerald G. Somers, University of Wisconsin, and Masumi Tsuda, Musashi University

Collection and Utilization of Job Vacancy Data in France, Jacques Chazelle, Ministry of Labor, France

Collection and Uses of Job Vacancy Statistics in Sweden, Per Holmberg, Bromma, Sweden

Collection and Use of Job Vacancy Data in the Netherlands, L. J. Niesten, Netherlands Ministry of Social Affairs and Public Health

III. Job Vacancy Surveys in the United States

Problems in the Collection of Data on Vacancies: Chicago Pilot Study, Elizabeth J. Slotkin, Illinois Bureau of Employment Security

Experimental Job Vacancy Survey Program of the United States Department of Labor, Irvin F. O. Wingeard, Bureau of Labor Statistics

Employment Service Operating Data as a Measure of Job Vacancies, Vladimir D. Chavrid and Harold Kuptzin, U.S. Employment Service

Conceptual and Measurement Problems in Job Vacancies: A Progress Report on the NICB Study, John G. Myers, National Industrial Conference Board, Inc.

The Time Dimension in the Collection of Job Vacancy Data, Robert Ferber and Neil Ford, University of Illinois

IV. Alternative Approaches to Measuring Job Vacancies

Job Openings and Help-Wanted Advertising as Measures of Cyclical Fluctuations in Unfilled Demand for Labor, Charlotte Boschan, National Bureau

An Evaluation of Private Employment Agencies as Sources of Job Vacancy Data, Eaton H. Conant, University of Chicago

The Relations Between Temporary Help Services and Job Vacancies: A Pilot Study, Mack A. Moore, Georgia Institute of Technology

VISITORS TO THE NATIONAL BUREAU

Economists, businessmen, government officials, and students visit the National Bureau to learn about its methods of work, organization, and research findings. Often they come from foreign countries. During 1964, individuals visited the National Bureau from some twenty-three countries: Australia, Bulgaria, Canada, Chile, El Salvador, France, Great Britain, Hungary, Iceland, India, Indonesia, Italy, Japan, Nepal, Northern Ireland, Pakistan, Poland, Singapore, Turkey, U.S.S.R., United Arab Republic, West Germany, and Yugoslavia. Also in 1964 and early 1965, at the conferences referred to above on national economic planning and on measurement and interpretation of job vacancies, papers were presented by economists from Canada, France, United Kingdom, Japan, Sweden, and the Netherlands.

PART VI

Directors, Officers, and Research Staff

At the 1965 Annual Meeting of the National Bureau, Walter W. Heller, Geoffrey H. Moore, William Newman, and Gus Tyler were elected Directors at Large.

Officers elected were Frank W. Fetter, Chairman; Arthur F. Burns, President; Theodore O. Yntema, Vice-President; Donald B. Woodward, Treasurer; Solomon Fabricant, Director of Research; Geoffrey H. Moore and Hal B. Lary, Associate Directors of Research; and William J. Carson, Executive Director and Secretary.

In view of Solomon Fabricant's wish to be relieved of his administrative responsibilities, the Board elected Geoffrey H. Moore as Director of Research, effective June 1. Dr. Fabricant will continue as a member of the research staff.

Owing to the impending retirement of William J. Carson, Douglas H. Eldridge was appointed Executive Director effective on or about July 1, 1965. Dr. Carson will continue to serve as Secretary of the Board through February 1966.

Joseph W. Conard, member of the research staff since 1960, died on April 5, 1965. A resolution adopted by the Executive Committee reads in part: "He will long be remembered at the National Bureau for his patient, interested attitude toward the work of others. He was a man who believed in, and achieved much by, friendly persuasion. His eagerness to benefit from criticism of his own work, and the care with which he evaluated evidence and stated his conclusions, marked him as a scholar."

Jack M. Guttentag, University of Pennsylvania, was appointed a member of the research staff in 1964.

George R. Morrison, Cornell University, was appointed a research fellow for the academic year 1964-65. Michael Michaely, Hebrew University, and George Hempel, Washington University, were appointed research fellows for 1965-66. These appointments mark the resumption of a program that began in 1930 and continued for many years, under which the National Bureau appointed one or two research fellows (formerly, research associates) to its staff for one year. A recent grant from the Alfred P. Sloan Foundation has provided funds sufficient for a period of three years.

Research fellowships are available to men or women with university position, ordinarily with the rank of assistant or associate professor and with the Ph.D. degree. A year of research in an institution devoted entirely to this activity, coupled with freedom from teaching responsibilities, can be of great benefit to the college teacher, to his college when he returns, and to economic science.

At the National Bureau, research fellows are provided with needed research assistance, computer facilities, clerical and editorial assistance, and, most important, with an opportunity to discuss their plans and findings with colleagues interested and experienced in research. Research topics are selected by mutual agreement and are limited to undertakings related to the National Bureau's program and in keeping with its research policy. Stipends are adjusted according to the individual's annual earnings, with an allowance for differences in living costs and costs of moving.

The National Bureau's research assistants form an able and devoted corps who contribute greatly to the quality and efficiency of the Bureau's studies. The custom of having members of the research staff address seminars held for the research assistants, many of whom are graduate students, was continued in 1964. The seminars, arranged by Charlotte Boschan, dealt with cyclical behavior of money, variable-span diffusion indexes, investment in human capital and the distribution of income, and productivity in the service industries.

The National Bureau's research program benefits from the collaborative efforts of many individuals and groups. The Board of Directors governs its policies, selects its officers, approves research undertakings, and reviews each report before publication. Advisory and exploratory committees—such as those for the studies of consumer finance, interest rates, capital markets, pension systems, tax policies for economic growth, banking markets and bank structure, and measurement and interpretation of job vacancies—aid in the planning of research projects and review the progress of the investigations. The Universities-National Bureau Committee for Economic Research, the Conference on Research in Income and Wealth, and other committees plan and organize conferences, securing the cooperation of many specialists on the subjects selected. Finally, many individuals who are no longer on the research staff nonetheless undertake to revise or otherwise complete reports that will in due course be issued by the National Bureau. The voluntary services of all these collaborators, who in the aggregate far outnumber the National Bureau's own personnel, play a vital part in each year's achievement.

A note about each of the authors of National Bureau studies completed in 1964 or in process is given at the end of this report. Of the 78 individuals listed there, 58 are faculty members at 30 universities and colleges in the United States.

PART VII

Finances and Sources of Support

During 1964 the National Bureau spent $1,402,045 on its research and related operations. Approximately 52 per cent of the expenditures was financed from general funds and 48 per cent from grants for specific studies. The results of all studies, regardless of the source of funds, are made available to the public at large through the National Bureau's publications.

Funds for the support of the work of the National Bureau come from many sources, among them philanthropic foundations, business associations, public agencies, companies, labor organizations, and individuals. In addition, many valuable services are contributed to the National Bureau's work.

Philanthropic foundations and similar sources whose grants supported studies planned, carried on, or completed in 1964 include the Carnegie Corporation, the Maurice and Laura Falk Foundation, the Ford Foundation, the Rockefeller Foundation, the Rockefeller Brothers Fund, the Russell Sage Foundation, the Scherman Foundation, and the Alfred P. Sloan Foundation. About 19 per cent of the income used in 1964 was provided by direct grants from these sources, and approximately 22 per cent was provided by interest and dividend income on capital-sum grants from foundations.

Business associations and other organizations providing funds for specific studies and other support include the American Bankers Association, the Automobile Manufacturers Association, the Life Insurance Association of America, the Mortgage Bankers Association, the United States Savings and Loan League, and the National Association of Mutual Savings Banks. Grants from these sources provided 13 per cent of total income used in 1964.

Public agencies from which income was received in 1964 include the National Science Foundation and the Office of Manpower, Automation and Training of the Department of Labor. Funds from these sources provided 8 per cent of the National Bureau's total income.

The National Committee on Government

Finance, through the Brookings Institution, cooperated with the National Bureau in sponsoring two research conferences on tax policies for economic growth and participated in providing funds toward their financing.

Cash contributions and subscriptions for general support of the National Bureau's work received from companies, labor organizations, individuals, libraries, and the like totaled $357,553 in 1964, about 25 per cent of the total budget. Another 11 per cent was supplied by companies contributing to the support of specific studies, and 2 per cent came from publication sales.

New grants received in 1964 included one from the National Science Foundation to supplement an earlier grant for the comparative study of prices and price trends. The Office of Manpower, Automation and Training, Department of Labor, made a grant for a conference on the measurement and interpretation of job vacancies.

The Sloan Foundation made a five-year grant for a study of productivity, employment, and price levels. The Life Insurance Association of America made a grant to provide further support for the study of interest rates.

Grants from several companies provided support for specific projects, among them the study of consumer finance, the study of short-term economic forecasting, and the study of applications of electronic computers to economic research. Many companies, banks, and public agencies contributed data, research materials, and other resources for use by the National Bureau in its investigations.

Information on how to make cash contributions to the support of the National Bureau and how to obtain its publications is given on pages 116-117. A full list of publications issued to date begins on page 105. A catalogue is available on request to the National Bureau.

AUTHORS OF STUDIES COMPLETED OR IN PROCESS DURING 1964-65

MOSES ABRAMOVITZ, A.B. Harvard, Ph.D. Columbia; prof. econ. Stanford; NBER since 1938; pubs.: *Inventories and Business Cycles* (1950); *The Nature and Significance of Kuznets Cycles* (1961).

THOMAS R. ATKINSON, B.A. Denison, M.A., Ph.D. Wisconsin; econ. Scudder, Stevens & Clark; NBER since 1949; pub.: *The Pattern of Financial Asset Ownership* (1956).

MORRIS BECK, B.A. Penn State, M.A., Ph.D. Columbia; prof. econ. Rutgers; NBER since 1962; pubs.: "Ability to Shift the Corporate Income Tax" *(National Tax J.,* Sept. 1950); *Property Taxation and Urban Land Use in Northeastern New Jersey* (1963).

GARY S. BECKER, A.B. Princeton, Ph.D. Chicago; prof. econ. Columbia; NBER since 1957; pubs.: *The Economics of Discrimination* (1957); *Human Capital* (1964).

CHARLOTTE BOSCHAN, B.S. N.Y.U., M.A. Columbia; NBER since 1952; pubs.: "Economic Projections to 1975," in *The Economy of New Jersey* (1958); "Application of Electronic Computers to Business Cycle Research" (with G. Bry, ASA Proceedings, 1960).

PHILIP J. BOURQUE, Ph.D. Pennsylvania; prof. bus. econ. Washington; NBER since 1962; pubs.: "The Domestic Importance of Foreign Trade of the U.S." *(RES,* Nov. 1954); "Regional Patterns of Seasonality in the Labor Force and Its Components" *(Q. Rev. Econ. and Bus.,* Nov. 1962).

GEORGE K. BRINEGAR, B.Ed, Ill. Normal U., M.S., Ph.D. Chicago; NBER since 1965; pubs.: "Fragmentation of Agricultural Economics Research" *(JFE,* Aug. 1959); "Income Savings Balances and Net Saving" *(RES,* Feb. 1963).

WILLIAM H. BROWN, JR., B.A., Ph.D. Yale; assoc. prof. econ. Swarthmore; NBER since 1960; pubs.: "Innovation in the Machine Tool Industry" *(QJE,* Aug. 1957); *Planning Municipal Investment* (with C. H. Gilbert, 1961).

GERHARD BRY, Ph.D. Columbia; prof. econ. N.Y.U.; NBER since 1940; pubs.: *The Average Workweek as an Economic Indicator* (1959); *Wages in Germany, 1871-1945* (1960).

ARTHUR F. BURNS, A.B., A.M., Ph.D. Columbia; John Bates Clark prof. econ. Columbia; NBER since 1930; pubs.: *Measuring Business Cycles* (with W. Mitchell, 1946); *Frontiers of Economic Knowledge* (1954).

PHILIP CAGAN, A.A. U.C.L.A., M.A., Ph.D. Chicago; prof. econ. Brown; NBER since 1953; pubs.: "Monetary Dynamics of Hyperinflation," in *Studies in the Quantity Theory of Money* (1956); *Determinants and Effects of Changes in the Stock of Money, 1875-1960* (1965).

AVERY B. COHAN, B.A. Cornell, M.A., Ph.D. Columbia; prof. fin. North Carolina; NBER 1942 and since 1961; pubs.: *Private Placements and Public Offerings* (1961); "The Theory of the Firm: A View on Methodology" *(J. Business,* July 1963).

ROSANNE COLE, A.B. Miami; NBER since 1956.

JOSEPH W. CONARD, B.A. Grinnell, M.A., Ph.D. California (Berkeley); prof. econ. Swarthmore; NBER since 1960; pubs.: *An Introduction to the Theory of Interest* (1959); "The Behavior of Interest Rates: A Progress Report" (NBER, in prep.). Dr. Conard died on April 5, 1965.

JON CUNNYNGHAM, B.A. Oberlin, Ph.D. Chicago; assoc. prof. econ. Columbia; NBER since 1963; pub.: *The Spectral Analysis of Economic Time Series* (1963).

DOUGLAS B. DIAMOND, M.S. Maryland, Chicago; U.S. government; NBER since 1964; pub.: *Agricultural Statistics of the USSR* (1955).

FRANK G. DICKINSON, B.A. Illinois, M.A. Penn State, Ph.D. Illinois; prof. econ. Northern Illinois; NBER since 1959; pubs.; "Public Works and Cyclical Unemployment" *(Annals Am. Acad. Pol. & Soc. Sci.* Suppl., Sept. 1928); *Philanthropy and Public Policy* (editor, 1962).

JAMES S. EARLEY, B.A. Antioch, M.A., Ph.D. Wisconsin; prof. econ., chmn. dept. econ. Wisconsin; NBER since 1959; pubs.: *Pricing for Profit and Growth* (1957, 2nd ed., 1961); "Marginal Policies of 'Excellently Managed' Companies" *(AER,* March 1956).

NOTE: Authors of conference papers or committee reports published or in preparation during 1964 are not included. The entry "NBER since..." does not necessarily mean either continuous or full-time service at the National Bureau.

RICHARD A. EASTERLIN, M.E. Stevens Institute, A.M., Ph.D. Pennsylvania; prof. econ. Pennsylvania; NBER since 1955; pubs.: *Population Redistribution and Economic Growth, United States, 1870-1950*, I, II (coauth., 1957, 1960); *The American Baby Boom in Historical Perspective* (1962).

SOLOMON FABRICANT, B.C.S. N.Y.U., B.S. C.C.N.Y., A.M., Ph.D. Columbia; prof. econ. N.Y.U.; NBER since 1930; pubs.: *Capital Consumption and Adjustment* (1938); *The Trend of Government Activity in the United States since 1900* (1952).

RENDIGS FELS, A.B., Ph.D. Harvard, A.M. Columbia; prof., chmn. dept. econ. and bus. Vanderbilt; NBER since 1964; pubs.: *American Business Cycles, 1865-1897* (1959); *Challenge to the American Economy* (1961).

LYLE P. FETTIG, B.S., M.S. Michigan State, A.M., Ph.D. Chicago; asst. prof. agri. econ. Illinois; NBER since 1965; pubs.: "Adjusting Farm Tractor Prices for Quality Changes, 1950-1962" *(JFE,* Aug. 1963); "Use of Short-Term Agricultural Credit in Illinois" *(Ill. Agric. Econ.,* 1965).

EDGAR R. FIEDLER, B.B.A. Wisconsin, M.B.A. Michigan; econ. dept. Bankers Trust Co.; NBER since 1965; pubs.: "Long-Lead and Short-Lead Indexes of Business Indicators" (ASA, *Proc. Bus. & Econ. Stat. Sec.,* 1962); "Keeping Posted on Profits" *(Fin. Anal. J.,* May-June 1964).

ALBERT FISHLOW, B.A. Pennsylvania, Ph.D. Harvard; assoc. prof. econ. California (Berkeley); NBER since 1963; pubs.: "Trustee Savings Banks, 1817-1861" *(J. Econ. Hist.,* March 1961); *American Railroads and the Transformation of the Ante-Bellum Economy* (Cambridge, 1965).

MILTON FRIEDMAN, B.A. Rutgers, M.A. Chicago, Ph.D. Columbia; prof. econ. Chicago; NBER since 1937; pubs.: *A Theory of the Consumption Function* (1957); *A Monetary History of the United States, 1867-1960* (with A. J. Schwartz, 1963).

VICTOR R. FUCHS, B.S. N.Y.U., M.A., Ph.D. Columbia; NBER since 1962; pubs.: *Concepts and Cases in Economic Analysis* (with A. Warner, 1958); *Changes in the Location of Manufacturing in the United States since 1929* (1962).

HOURMOUZIS G. GEORGIADIS, B.A., Ph.D. Cornell; Jonathan Dickinson Preceptor, asst. prof. econ. Princeton; NBER since 1961; pub.: *Balance of Payments Equilibrium* (1963).

HARRY J. GILMAN, A.M., Ph.D. Chicago; res. econ. Center for Naval Analyses; NBER since 1963; pubs.: "The White-Nonwhite Employment Differential," in *Conference on the Economics of Urban Human Resources* (1963).

RAYMOND W. GOLDSMITH, Ph.D. Berlin; prof. econ. Yale; vice-pres. OECD Development Centre; NBER since 1951; pubs.: *Financial Intermediaries in the American Economy* (1958); *Studies in the National Balance Sheet of the United States* (with R. E. Lipsey, 1963).

MANUEL GOTTLIEB, B.A. Minnesota, M.A. California (Berkeley), Ph.D. Harvard; assoc. prof. econ. Wisconsin; NBER since 1961; pubs.: "Theory of an Economic System" *(AER,* May 1953); "Value and Price in Industrial Markets" *(EJ,* Mar. 1959).

JACK M. GUTTENTAG, B.S. Purdue, M.S., Ph.D. Columbia; assoc. prof. fin. Pennsylvania; NBER since 1961; pubs.: "The Short Cycle in Residential Construction, 1946-59" *(AER,* June 1961); *The Federal National Mortgage Association* (1963).

CHALLIS A. HALL, JR., B.S. Kansas, A.M., Ph.D. Harvard; prof. econ. Yale; NBER since 1961; pubs.: *Effects of Taxation on Executive Compensation and Retirement Plans* (1951); *Fiscal Policy for Stable Growth* (1960).

JOHN HERZOG, B.S., Ph.D. California (Berkeley); assoc. prof. comm. Wisconsin; NBER since 1963; pubs.: *The Dynamics of Large-Scale Housebuilding* (1963); "Investor Experiences in Corporate Securities—A New Technique for Measurement" *(J. Fin.,* Mar. 1964).

DANIEL M. HOLLAND, B.A., Ph.D. Columbia; prof. fin. M.I.T.; NBER since 1949; pubs.: *The Income-Tax Burden on Stockholders* (1958); *Dividends Under the Income Tax* (1962).

THOR HULTGREN, A.B., M.A. Columbia; vis. fac. member, Wisconsin; NBER since 1940; pubs.: *American Transportation in Prosperity and Depression* (1948); *Changes in Labor Cost During Cycles in Production and Business* (1960).

DONALD P. JACOBS, Ph.D. Columbia; assoc. prof. fin. Northwestern; NBER since 1965; pubs.: "Sources and Costs of Funds of Large Sales Finance Companies," in *Consumer Instalment Credit* (1957); "The Framework of Commercial Bank Regulation—An Appraisal" *(Nat. Bank R.,* 1964).

D. GALE JOHNSON, B.S. Iowa State, M.S. Wisconsin, Ph.D. Iowa State; prof. econ., dean div. of soc. sci. Chicago; NBER since 1958; pubs.: *Forward Prices for Agriculture* (1947); *Agriculture and Trade* (1950).

F. THOMAS JUSTER, B.S. Rutgers, Ph.D. Columbia; NBER since 1957; pubs.: *Consumer Expectations, Plans, and Purchases* (1960); *Anticipations and Purchases: An Analysis of Consumer Behavior* (1964).

ARCADIUS KAHAN, M.A., Ph.D. Rutgers; assoc. prof. econ. Chicago; NBER since 1961; pubs.: *Soviet Agriculture, Structure and Growth* (1959); *The Soviet Agricultural Program: An Evaluation of the 1965 Goals* (with D. G. Johnson, 1962).

C. HARRY KAHN, B.A. Vanderbilt, M.A., Ph.D. Wisconsin; prof. econ. Rutgers; NBER since 1952; pubs.: *Personal Deductions in the Federal Income Tax* (1960); *Business and Professional Income Under the Personal Income Tax* (1964).

JOHN W. KENDRICK, A.B., M.A. North Carolina, Ph.D. George Washington; University Professor econ. Connecticut; NBER since 1954; pubs.: *Productivity Trends in the United States* (1961); *Measuring the Nation's Wealth* (coauth., 1964).

REUBEN A. KESSEL, M.B.A., Ph.D. Chicago; assoc. prof. bus. econ. Chicago; NBER since 1961; pubs.: "Inflation-Caused Wealth Redistribution" (*AER*, Mar. 1956); *The Cyclical Behavior of the Term Structure of Interest Rates* (1965).

PHILIP A. KLEIN, B.A., M.A. Texas, Ph.D. California (Berkeley); assoc. prof. econ. Penn. State; NBER since 1956; pubs.: "Changes in the Quality of Consumer Instalment Credit," in *Consumer Instalment Credit* (1957); *Financial Adjustments to Unemployment* (1965).

IRVING B. KRAVIS, B.S., A.M., Ph.D. Pennsylvania; prof. econ. Pennsylvania; NBER since 1962; pubs.: *The Structure of Income; Some Quantitative Essays* (1962); *Domestic Interests and International Obligations: A Study of Trade Safeguards* (1963).

ERNEST KURNOW, B.S., M.S. C.C.N.Y., Ph.D. N.Y.U.; prof. bus. stat. N.Y.U.; NBER since 1963; pubs.: *Statistics for Business Decisions* (coauth., 1959); *Theory and Measurement of Rent* (coauth., 1961).

HAL B. LARY, lic. ès. sc. pol. Geneva; NBER since 1960; pubs.: *The United States in the World Economy* (1943); *Problems of the United States as World Trader and Banker* (1963).

ROBERT E. LIPSEY, B.A., M.A., Ph.D. Columbia; NBER since 1945; pubs.: *Price and Quantity Trends in the Foreign Trade of the United States* (1963); *Studies in the National Balance Sheet of the United States* (with R. W. Goldsmith, 1963).

RUTH P. MACK, A.B. Barnard, Ph.D. Columbia; Institute of Public Administration; NBER since 1941; pubs.: *Flow of Business Funds and Consumer Purchasing Power* (1940); *Consumption and Business Fluctuations* (1956).

DAVID MEISELMAN, A.B. Boston, M.A., Ph.D. Chicago; Office of the Comptroller; NBER since 1955; pubs.: *The Term Structure of Interest Rates* (1962); "The Relative Stability of Monetary Velocity and the Investment Multiplier in the U.S., 1897-1958" (with M. Friedman, in *Stabilization Policies*, 1964).

WALTHER P. MICHAEL, B.S. Columbia; asst. prof. econ. Ohio State; NBER since 1954; pub.: "International Capital Movements, 1950-54" (in prep.).

MICHAEL MICHAELY, M.A. Hebrew (Jerusalem), Ph.D. Johns Hopkins; chmn. dept. econ. Hebrew (Jerusalem); NBER since 1965; pubs.: *Concentration in International Trade* (1962); *Foreign Trade and Capital Imports in Israel* (1963).

ROGER F. MILLER, B.A. Princeton, M.B.A. Pennsylvania, Ph.D. California (Berkeley); assoc. prof. econ. Wisconsin; NBER since 1962; pubs.: "A Note on the Theory of Investment and Production" (*QJE*, Nov. 1959); "The Theory of Household Saving" (*RES*, Feb. 1963).

JACOB MINCER, B.A. Emory, Ph.D. Columbia; prof. econ. Columbia; NBER since 1960; pubs.: "Investment in Human Capital and Personal Income Distribution" (*JPE*, Aug. 1958); "Labor Force Participation of Married Women," in *Aspects of Labor Economics* (1962).

ILSE MINTZ, doc. rer. pol. Vienna, Ph.D. Columbia; prof. econ. Columbia; NBER since 1949; pubs.: *Deterioration in the Quality of Foreign Bonds* (1951); *American Exports During Business Cycles* (1961).

GEOFFREY H. MOORE, B.S., M.S. Rutgers, Ph.D. Harvard; NBER since 1939; pubs.: *Production of Industrial Materials in World Wars I and II* (1944); *Business Cycle Indicators* (editor, 1961).

GEORGE R. MORRISON, Ph.D. Chicago; asst. prof. econ. Cornell; NBER since 1964; pubs.: "Deposit Structure, the Price Level, and Bank Earnings" (*NBR*, Dec. 1964); *Time Deposit Growth and the Employment of Bank Funds* (1965).

WALLACE P. MORS, Ph.B., A.M., Ph.D. Chicago, C.P.A. Illinois; prof., chmn. dept. fin. Babson Institute; NBER since 1960; pubs.: "Consumer Instalment Credit Insurance" *(Ins. Law J.,* May 1956); "Recent Trends in State Regulation of Instalment Credit" *(J. Fin.,* May 1960).

ROGER F. MURRAY, B.A. Yale, M.B.A., Ph.D. N.Y.U., S. Sloan Colt prof. banking and fin. Grad. Sch. of Bus., Columbia; NBER since 1958; pubs.: *Pensions: Problems and Trends* (contrib., 1955); *Business Loans of American Commercial Banks* (contrib., 1959).

RALPH L. NELSON, B.S. Minnesota, A.M., Ph.D. Columbia; assoc. prof. econ. C.U.N.Y.; NBER since 1955; pubs.: *Merger Movements in American Industry* (1959); *Concentration in the Manufacturing Industries: A Midcentury Report* (1963).

G. WARREN NUTTER, A.B., A.M., Ph.D. Chicago; prof., chmn. dept. econ. Virginia; NBER since 1954; pubs.: *Extent and Growth of Enterprise Monopoly in the U.S.* (1951); *Growth of Industrial Production in the Soviet Union* (1962).

DORIS PRESTON, B.S. California (Berkeley); NBER since 1961.

LAWRENCE S. RITTER, B.A. Indiana, M.A., Ph.D. Wisconsin; prof. fin. N.Y.U.; NBER since 1963; pubs.: "The Structure of the Flow of Funds Accounts" *(J. Fin.,* May 1963); "The Role of Money in Keynesian Theory," in *Banking and Monetary Studies* (1963).

ANNA JACOBSON SCHWARTZ, B.A. Barnard, M.A., Ph.D. Columbia; NBER since 1941; pubs.: *Growth and Fluctuation of the British Economy, 1790-1850* (coauth., 1953); *A Monetary History of the United States, 1867-1960* (with M. Friedman, 1963).

DAVID SCHWARTZMAN, B.A. McGill, Ph.D. California; assoc. prof. econ. New School for Social Research; NBER since 1963; pubs.: "The Effect of Monopoly on Price" *(JPE,* Aug. 1959); "Uncertainty and the Size of the Firm" *(Economica,* Aug. 1963).

MARTIN H. SEIDEN, B.A. C.C.N.Y., M.A., Ph.D. Columbia; lect. econ. C.U.N.Y.; econ. consultant; NBER since 1959; pubs.: *The Quality of Trade Credit* (1964); *Economic Analysis of CATV and Television Broadcasting* (1965).

RICHARD T. SELDEN, B.A. Chicago, M.A. Columbia; Ph.D. Chicago; prof. econ. Cornell; NBER since 1959; pubs.: *The Postwar Rise in the Velocity of Money* (1962); *Trends and Cycles in the Commercial Paper Market* (1963).

LAWRENCE H. SELTZER, A.B., A.M., Ph.D. Michigan; prof. econ. Wayne State; NBER since 1941; pubs.: *A Financial History of the American Automobile Industry* (1928); *The Nature and Tax Treatment of Capital Gains and Losses* (1950).

ELI SHAPIRO, A.B. Brooklyn, A.M., Ph.D. Columbia; prof. fin. Harvard; NBER since 1955; pubs.: *Money and Banking* (with Steiner and Solomon, 4th ed., 1958); *The Measurement of Corporate Sources and Uses of Funds* (with D. Meiselman, 1964).

ROBERT P. SHAY, B.S., M.A., Ph.D. Virginia; prof. banking Columbia; NBER since 1959; pubs.: *New-Automobile Finance Rates, 1924-62* (1963); *Consumer Sensitivity to Finance Rates* (with F. T. Juster, 1964).

JULIUS SHISKIN, A.B., A.M. Rutgers; chief econ. stat. Bureau of Census; NBER since 1938; pubs.: *Electronic Computers and Business Indicators* (1957); *Signals of Recession and Recovery* (1961).

PAUL F. SMITH, A.B. Chicago, M.A. Northwestern, Ph.D. American U.; assoc. prof. fin. Pennsylvania; NBER since 1960; pubs.: "Response of Consumer Loans to General Credit Conditions" *(AER,* Sept. 1958); *Consumer Credit Costs, 1949-59* (1964).

THOMAS M. STANBACK, JR., B.S. North Carolina, M.B.A. Harvard, Ph.D. Duke; assoc. prof. econ. N.Y.U.; NBER since 1955; pubs.: "The Textile Cycle: Characteristics and Contributing Factors," *(Southern Econ. J.,* Oct. 1958); *Postwar Cycles in Manufacturers' Inventories* (1962).

GEORGE J. STIGLER, B.B.A. Washington, M.B.A. Northwestern, Ph.D. Chicago; Walgreen prof. Amer. Instit. Chicago; NBER since 1942; pub.: *Capital and Rates of Return in Manufacturing Industries* (1963).

LEO TROY, B.A. Penn State, Ph.D. Columbia; assoc. prof. econ. Rutgers; NBER since 1953; pubs.: *Distribution of Union Membership among the States* (1957); *Union Organization in New Jersey* (1965).

NORMAN B. TURE, M.A. Chicago; NBER since 1961; pubs.: *Federal Revenue System: Facts and Problems* (1961); "Tax Reform: Depreciation Problems" *(AER,* May 1963).

JEAN ALEXANDER WILBURN, B.A. California (Berkeley), M.A., Ph.D. Columbia; asst. prof. econ. Barnard; NBER since 1963.

HERBERT B. WOOLLEY, A.B. Stanford, Ph.D. Harvard; chief econ. adv., Supreme Planning Board, Saudi Arabia; NBER since 1953; pubs.: "The General Elasticity of Demand" *(Econometrica,* July 1947); "Transactions between World Areas in 1951" *(RES* Supp., Feb. 1958).

VICTOR ZARNOWITZ, A.B., Ph.D. Heidelberg; prof. econ. and fin. Chicago; NBER since 1952; pubs.: "The Timing of Manufacturers' Orders During Business Cycles," in *Business Cycle Indicators* (1961); *Unfilled Orders, Price Changes, and Business Fluctuations* (1962).

National Bureau Publications

Instructions for ordering are on page 117.

Annotated catalogues of publications are available on request.

Abbreviations

CUP — Available from Columbia University Press
2960 Broadway, New York, N. Y.

PUP — Available from Princeton University Press
Princeton, New Jersey

UM — Available from University Microfilms, Inc.
313 N. First St., Ann Arbor, Mich.

BOOKS

GENERAL SERIES

*1 *Income in the United States: Its Amount and Distribution, 1909-1919. I, Summary*
Wesley C. Mitchell, Willford I. King, Frederick R. Macaulay, and Oswald W. Knauth
1921, 168 pp.

*2 *Income in the United States: Its Amount and Distribution, 1909-1919. II, Detailed Report*
Wesley C. Mitchell (ed.), Willford I. King, Frederick R. Macaulay, and Oswald W. Knauth
1922, 454 pp.

*3 *Distribution of Income by States in 1919*
Oswald W. Knauth   1922, 35 pp.

*4 *Business Cycles and Unemployment*
Committee of the President's Conference on Unemployment, and a Special Staff of the National Bureau   UM, 1923, 445 pp.

*5 *Employment Hours and Earnings in Prosperity and Depression, United States, 1920-1922*
Willford Isbell King   UM, 1923, 2nd ed., 151 pp.

*6 *The Growth of American Trade Unions, 1880-1923*
Leo Wolman   1924, 170 pp.

*7 *Income in the Various States: Its Sources and Distribution, 1919, 1920, and 1921*
Maurice Leven   1925, 306 pp.

*8 *Business Annals*
Willard Long Thorp   UM, 1926, 380 pp.

9 *Migration and Business Cycles*
Harry Jerome   CUP, 1926, 258 pp., $2.50

10 *Business Cycles: The Problem and Its Setting*
Listed also under Studies in Business Cycles
Wesley C. Mitchell   CUP, 1927, 511 pp., $5.00

*11 *The Behavior of Prices*
Frederick C. Mills   1927, 598 pp.

12 *Trends in Philanthropy: A Study in a Typical American City*
Willford Isbell King   CUP, 1928, 78 pp., $1.00

*13 *Recent Economic Changes in the United States*
Committee on Recent Economic Changes of the President's Conference on Unemployment, and a Special Staff of the National Bureau
UM, 1929, 2 vols., 986 pp.

*14 *International Migrations. I, Statistics*
Imre Ferenczi (compiled on behalf of the International Labour Office, Walter F. Willcox, ed.)   UM, 1929, 1112 pp.

*15 *The National Income and Its Purchasing Power*
Willford Isbell King   UM, 1930, 394 pp.

*Out of print.

*16 *Corporation Contributions to Organized Community Welfare Services*
Pierce Williams and Frederick E. Croxton
UM, 1930, 347 pp.

*17 *Planning and Control of Public Works*
Leo Wolman   UM, 1930, 292 pp.

*18 *International Migrations. II, Interpretations*
Walter F. Willcox (ed.)   UM, 1931, 715 pp.

*19 *The Smoothing of Time Series*
Frederick R. Macaulay   UM, 1931, 172 pp.

20 *The Purchase of Medical Care through Fixed Periodic Payment*
Pierce Williams   CUP, 1932, 324 pp., $3.00

*21 *Economic Tendencies in the United States: Aspects of Pre-War and Post-War Changes*
Frederick C. Mills   1932, 659 pp.

22 *Seasonal Variations in Industry and Trade*
Simon Kuznets   CUP, 1933, 479 pp., $4.00

†23 *Production Trends in the United States since 1870*
Arthur F. Burns   1934, 395 pp.

†24 *Strategic Factors in Business Cycles*
John Maurice Clark   1934, 253 pp.

25 *German Business Cycles, 1924-1933*
Carl T. Schmidt   CUP, 1934, 302 pp., $2.50

26 *Industrial Profits in the United States*
Ralph C. Epstein   CUP, 1934, 687 pp., $5.00

*27 *Mechanization in Industry*
Harry Jerome   1934, 515 pp.

28 *Corporate Profits as Shown by Audit Reports*
W. A. Paton   CUP, 1935, 162 pp., $1.25

*29 *Public Works in Prosperity and Depression*
Arthur D. Gayer   UM, 1935, 480 pp.

*30 *Ebb and Flow in Trade Unionism*
Leo Wolman   1936, 268 pp.

*31 *Prices in Recession and Recovery: A Survey of Recent Changes*
Frederick C. Mills   1936, 596 pp.

*32 *National Income and Capital Formation, 1919-1935*
Simon Kuznets   UM, 1937, 96 pp.

33 *Some Theoretical Problems Suggested by the Movements of Interest Rates, Bond Yields and Stock Prices in the United States since 1856*
Frederick R. Macaulay
CUP, 1938, 604 pp., $5.00
The Social Sciences and the Unknown Future, introductory chapter from the above CUP, 25¢

*34 *Commodity Flow and Capital Formation, Volume I*
Simon Kuznets   UM, 1938, 514 pp.

*35 *Capital Consumption and Adjustment*
Solomon Fabricant   UM, 1938, 291 pp.

*36 *The Structure of Manufacturing Production: A Cross-Section View*
Charles A. Bliss   UM, 1939, 248 pp.

*37 *The International Gold Standard Reinterpreted, 1914-1934*
William Adams Brown, Jr.
UM, 1940, 2 vols., 1470 pp.

*38 *Residential Real Estate: Its Economic Position as Shown by Values, Rents, Family Incomes, Financing, and Construction, Together with Estimates for All Real Estate*
David L. Wickens   UM, 1941, 327 pp.

*39 *The Output of Manufacturing Industries, 1899-1937*
Solomon Fabricant   UM, 1940, 708 pp.

40 *National Income and Its Composition, 1919-1938*
Simon Kuznets   CUP, 1941, 1019 pp., $6.00

*41 *Employment in Manufacturing, 1899-1939: An Analysis of Its Relation to the Volume of Production*
Solomon Fabricant   1942, 381 pp.

*42 *American Agriculture, 1899-1939: A Study of Output, Employment and Productivity*
Harold Barger and Hans H. Landsberg
UM, 1942, 462 pp.

*43 *The Mining Industries, 1899-1939: A Study of Output, Employment and Productivity*
Harold Barger and Sam H. Schurr
UM, 1944, 474 pp.

44 *National Product in Wartime*
Simon Kuznets   CUP, 1945, 166 pp., $2.00

45 *Income from Independent Professional Practice*
Milton Friedman and Simon Kuznets
CUP, 1945, 632 pp., $5.50

*46 *National Product since 1869*
Simon Kuznets   1946, 256 pp.

47 *Output and Productivity in the Electric and Gas Utilities, 1899-1942*
Jacob Martin Gould CUP, 1946, 207 pp., $3.00

48 *Value of Commodity Output since 1869*
William Howard Shaw
CUP, 1947, 320 pp., $4.00

49 *Business Incorporations in the United States, 1800-1943*
George Heberton Evans, Jr.
CUP, 1948, 8¾ x 11¼, 192 pp., $6.00

*50 *The Statistical Agencies of the Federal Government: A Report to the Commission on Organization of the Executive Branch of the Government*
Frederick C. Mills and Clarence D. Long
UM, 1949, 215 pp.

51 *The Transportation Industries, 1899-1946: A Study of Output, Employment, and Productivity*
Harold Barger   CUP, 1951, 304 pp., $4.00

---

*Out of print.
†Available from Augustus M. Kelley, Bookseller, 24 East 22 Street, New York, N. Y. 10010

52 *Deterioration in the Quality of Foreign Bonds Issued in the United States, 1920-1930*
Ilse Mintz   CUP, 1951, 111 pp., $2.00

53 *Wesley Clair Mitchell: The Economic Scientist*
Arthur F. Burns (ed.)
          CUP, 1952, 396 pp., $4.00

*54 *A Study of Moneyflows in the United States*
Morris A. Copeland   1952, 620 pp.

55 *Shares of Upper Income Groups in Income and Savings*
Simon Kuznets   CUP, 1953, 766 pp., $9.00

*56 *The Trend of Government Activity in the United States since 1900*
Solomon Fabricant   1952, 286 pp.

57 *The Frontiers of Economic Knowledge*
Arthur F. Burns   PUP, 1954, 378 pp., $5.00

*58 *Distribution's Place in the American Economy since 1869*
Harold Barger   UM, 1955, 240 pp.

59 *Trends in Employment in the Service Industries*
George J. Stigler   PUP, 1956, 183 pp., $3.75

60 *The Growth of Public Employment in Great Britain*
Moses Abramovitz and Vera F. Eliasberg
          PUP, 1957, 164 pp., $3.75

61 *Concentration in Canadian Manufacturing Industries*
Gideon Rosenbluth PUP, 1957, 167 pp., $3.50

62 *The Demand and Supply of Scientific Personnel*
David M. Blank and George J. Stigler
          PUP, 1957, 219 pp., $4.00

63 *A Theory of the Consumption Function*
Milton Friedman   PUP, 1957, 259 pp., $4.75

64 *The National Economic Accounts of the United States: Review, Appraisal, and Recommendations*
National Accounts Review Committee

Report made at the request of the Bureau of the Budget and submitted in hearings before the Subcommittee on Economic Statistics of the Joint Economic Committee (85th Cong., 1st Sess.) in October 1957; reprinted from the published *Hearings*.
          CUP, 1958, 204 pp., paperbound, $2.50

65 *The Labor Force under Changing Income and Employment*
Clarence D. Long   PUP, 1958, 464 pp., $10.00

66 *Merger Movements in American Industry, 1895-1956*
Ralph L. Nelson
          PUP, UM, 1959, 198 pp., $5.00

67 *Wages and Earnings in the United States, 1860-1890*
Clarence D. Long   PUP, 1960, 186 pp., $4.00

68 *Wages in Germany, 1871-1945*
Gerhard Bry   PUP, 1960, 513 pp., $10.00

69 *Soviet Statistics of Physical Output of Industrial Commodities: Their Compilation and Quality*
Gregory Grossman   PUP, 1960, 167 pp., $4.50

70 *Real Wages in Manufacturing, 1890-1914*
Albert Rees   PUP, 1961, 179 pp., $3.75

71 *Productivity Trends in the United States*
John W. Kendrick   PUP, 1961, 682 pp., $12.50

72 *The Growth of Public Expenditure in the United Kingdom*
Alan T. Peacock and Jack Wiseman
          PUP, 1961, 244 pp., $5.00

73 *The Price Statistics of the Federal Government*
Report of the Price Statistics Review Committee
Report made at the request of the Bureau of the Budget and submitted in hearings before the Subcommittee on Economic Statistics of the Joint Economic Committee (87th Cong., 1st Sess.); reprinted from the *Hearings*.
          CUP, 1961, 518 pp., $1.50

74 *The Share of Top Wealth-Holders in National Wealth, 1922-56*
Robert J. Lampman PUP, 1962, 313 pp., $6.50

75 *Growth of Industrial Production in the Soviet Union*
G. Warren Nutter   PUP, 1962, 733 pp., $15.00

76 *Freight Transportation in the Soviet Union, Including Comparisons with the United States*
Ernest W. Williams, Jr.
          PUP, 1962, 242 pp., $4.50

77 *Diversification and Integration in American Industry*
Michael Gort   PUP, 1962, 259 pp., $5.00

78 *Capital and Rates of Return in Manufacturing Industries*
George J. Stigler   PUP, 1963, 242 pp., $5.00

79 *Anticipations and Purchases: An Analysis of Consumer Behavior*
F. Thomas Juster   PUP, 1964, 321 pp., $6.50

80 *Human Capital: A Theoretical and Empirical Analysis, with Special Reference to Education*
Gary S. Becker   CUP, 1964, 203 pp., $5.00

Studies in Business Cycles

1 *Business Cycles: The Problem and Its Setting*
Wesley C. Mitchell   CUP, 1927, 511 pp., $5.00

2 *Measuring Business Cycles*
Arthur F. Burns and Wesley C. Mitchell
          CUP, 1946, 587 pp., $5.00
Also available from Recording for the Blind, Inc., 121 East 58 Street, New York, N. Y.

3 *American Transportation in Prosperity and Depression*
Thor Hultgren   CUP, 1948, 431 pp., $5.00

4 *Inventories and Business Cycles, with Special Reference to Manufacturers' Inventories*
Moses Abramovitz   CUP, 1950, 668 pp., $6.00

5 *What Happens during Business Cycles: A Progress Report*
Wesley C. Mitchell   CUP, 1951, 417 pp., $5.00

---

*Out of print.

6 *Personal Income during Business Cycles*
Daniel Creamer   PUP, 1956, 208 pp., $4.00

7 *Consumption and Business Fluctuations: A Case Study of the Shoe, Leather, Hide Sequence*
Ruth P. Mack   CUP, 1956, 310 pp., $7.50

8 *International Financial Transactions and Business Cycles*
Oskar Morgenstern PUP, 1959, 624 pp., $12.00

9 *Federal Receipts and Expenditures During Business Cycles, 1879-1958*
John M. Firestone   PUP, 1960, 192 pp., $4.00

10 *Business Cycle Indicators*
Geoffrey H. Moore, Editor   PUP, 1961
Vol. I, 792 pp., $12.50
Vol. II, 196 pp., $ 4.50
Both vols., $15.00

11 *Postwar Cycles in Manufacturers' Inventories*
Thomas M. Stanback, Jr.
PUP, 1962, 160 pp., $2.00

12 *A Monetary History of the United States, 1867-1960*
Milton Friedman and Anna Jacobson Schwartz
PUP, 1963, 884 pp., $15.00
The Great Contraction, 1929-33, Chapter 7 from the above (order from PUP only)
1965, 162 pp., $1.95

13 *Determinants and Effects of Changes in the Stock of Money, 1875-1960*
Phillip Cagan   CUP, 1965, 396 pp., $10.00

STUDIES IN CAPITAL FORMATION AND FINANCING

1 *Capital Formation in Residential Real Estate: Trends and Prospects*
Leo Grebler, David M. Blank, and
Louis Winnick   PUP, 1956, 549 pp., $10.00

*2 *Capital in Agriculture: Its Formation and Financing since 1870*
Alvin S. Tostlebe   UM, 1957, 258 pp.

3 *Financial Intermediaries in the American Economy since 1900*
Raymond W. Goldsmith
PUP, 1958, 450 pp., $8.50

4 *Capital in Transportation, Communications, and Public Utilities: Its Formation and Financing*
Melville J. Ulmer   PUP, 1960, 577 pp., $12.00

5 *Postwar Market for State and Local Government Securities*
Roland I. Robinson   PUP, 1960, 251 pp., $5.00

6 *Capital in Manufacturing and Mining: Its Formation and Financing*
Daniel Creamer, Sergei Dobrovolsky, and Israel Borenstein
PUP, UM, 1960, 398 pp., $7.50

7 *Trends in Government Financing*
Morris A. Copeland PUP, 1961, 236 pp., $5.00

8 *The Postwar Residential Mortgage Market*
Saul B. Klaman   PUP, 1961, 332 pp., $7.50

9 *Capital in the American Economy: Its Formation and Financing*
Simon Kuznets   PUP, 1961, 693 pp., $12.00

10 *The National Wealth of the United States in the Postwar Period*
Raymond W. Goldsmith
PUP, 1962, 463 pp., $12.50

11 *Studies in the National Balance Sheet of the United States*   PUP, 1963
Vol. I, Raymond W. Goldsmith and Robert E. Lipsey   458 pp., $8.50
Vol. II, Raymond W. Goldsmith, Robert E. Lipsey, and Morris Mendelson 551 pp., $7.50
Both vols., $15.00

12 *The Flow of Capital Funds in the Postwar Economy*
Raymond W. Goldsmith
CUP, 1965, 338 pp., $7.50

TWENTY-FIFTH ANNIVERSARY SERIES

*1 *National Income: A Summary of Findings*
Simon Kuznets   UM, 1946, 154 pp.

*2 *Price-Quantity Interactions in Business Cycles*
Frederick C. Mills   UM, 1946, 152 pp.

*3 *Economic Research and the Development of Economic Science and Public Policy*
1946, 208 pp.

*4 *Trends in Output and Employment*
George J. Stigler   1947, 76 pp.

FISCAL STUDIES

*1 *Fiscal Planning for Total War*
William Leonard Crum, John F. Fennelly, and Lawrence Howard Seltzer   1942, 338 pp.

*2 *Taxable and Business Income*
Dan Throop Smith and J. Keith Butters
1949, 367 pp.

*3 *The Nature and Tax Treatment of Capital Gains and Losses*
Lawrence H. Seltzer   1951, 576 pp.

4 *Federal Grants and the Business Cycle*
James A. Maxwell CUP, 1952, 134 pp., $2.00

5 *The Income-Tax Burden on Stockholders*
Daniel M. Holland   PUP, 1958, 266 pp., $5.00

6 *Personal Deductions in the Federal Income Tax*
C. Harry Kahn   PUP, 1960, 266 pp., $5.00

---

*Out of print.

7 *Dividends Under the Income Tax*
  Daniel M. Holland   PUP, 1962, 206 pp., $4.50

8 *Business and Professional Income Under the Personal Income Tax*
  C. Harry Kahn   PUP, 1964, 208 pp., $4.00

Financial Research Program

I A Program of Financial Research

One: *Report of the Exploratory Committee on Financial Research*
Exploratory Committee on Financial Research
    CUP, 1937, 91 pp., $1.00

Two: *Inventory of Current Research on Financial Problems*
Exploratory Committee on Financial Research
    CUP, 1937, 261 pp., $1.50

II Studies in Consumer Instalment Financing

*1 *Personal Finance Companies and Their Credit Practices*
   Ralph A. Young and Associates
       UM, 1940, 192 pp.

*2 *Sales Finance Companies and Their Credit Practices*
   Wilbur C. Plummer and Ralph A. Young
       1940, 321 pp.

3 *Commercial Banks and Consumer Instalment Credit*
  John M. Chapman and Associates
      CUP, 1940, 342 pp., $3.00

*4 *Industrial Banking Companies and Their Credit Practices*
   Raymond J. Saulnier   UM, 1940, 213 pp.

*5 *Government Agencies of Consumer Instalment Credit*
   Joseph D. Coppock   1940, 238 pp.

6 *The Pattern of Consumer Debt, 1935-36: A Statistical Analysis*
  Blanche Bernstein   CUP, 1940, 255 pp., $2.50

7 *The Volume of Consumer Instalment Credit, 1929-38*
  Duncan McC. Holthausen in collaboration with Malcolm L. Merriam and Rolf Nugent
      CUP, 1940, 156 pp., $1.50

8 *Risk Elements in Consumer Instalment Financing*
  David Durand
      CUP, Technical Ed., 1941, 186 pp., $2.00

*9 *Consumer Instalment Credit and Economic Fluctuations*
   Gottfried Haberler   1942, 258 pp.

---
*Out of print.

10 *Comparative Operating Experience of Consumer Instalment Financing Agencies and Commercial Banks, 1929-41*
   Ernst A. Dauer   CUP, 1944, 239 pp., $3.00

11 *Consumer Credit Costs, 1949-59*
   Paul F. Smith   PUP, 1964, 179 pp., $4.50

III Studies in Business Financing

1 *Term Lending to Business*
  Neil H. Jacoby and Raymond J. Saulnier
      CUP, 1942, 180 pp., $2.00

*2 *Financing Small Corporations in Five Manufacturing Industries, 1926-36*
   Charles L. Merwin   UM, 1942, 189 pp.

*3 *Accounts Receivable Financing*
   Raymond J. Saulnier and Neil H. Jacoby
       UM, 1943, 172 pp.

*4 *The Financing of Large Corporations, 1920-39*
   Albert Ralph Koch   1943, 156 pp.

*5 *Financing Equipment for Commercial and Industrial Enterprise*
   Raymond J. Saulnier and Neil H. Jacoby
       1944, 110 pp.

6 *Financing Inventory of Field Warehouse Receipts*
  Neil H. Jacoby and Raymond J. Saulnier
      CUP, 1944, 104 pp., $1.50

*7 *The Pattern of Corporate Financial Structure: A Cross-Section View of Manufacturing, Mining, Trade and Construction, 1937*
   Walter A. Chudson   UM, 1945, 162 pp.

8 *Corporate Cash Balances, 1914-43: Manufacturing and Trade*
  Friedrich A. Lutz   CUP, 1945, 146 pp., $2.00

9 *Business Finance and Banking*
  Neil H. Jacoby and Raymond J. Saulnier
      CUP, 1947, 259 pp., $3.50

*10 *Corporate Income Retention, 1915-43*
    Sergei P. Dobrovolsky   1951, 140 pp.

IV Studies in Urban Mortgage Financing

1 *Urban Mortgage Lending by Life Insurance Companies*
  R. J. Saulnier   CUP, 1950, 201 pp., $2.50

*2 *The Impact of Government on Real Estate Finance in the United States*
   Miles L. Colean   1950, 189 pp.

3 *Urban Real Estate Markets: Characteristics and Financing*
  Ernest M. Fisher   CUP, 1951, 207 pp., $3.00

4 *History and Policies of the Home Owners' Loan Corporation*
  C. Lowell Harriss   CUP, 1951, 223 pp., $3.00

5 *Commercial Bank Activities in Urban Mortgage Financing*
  Carl F. Behrens   CUP, 1952, 150 pp., $2.50

6 *Urban Mortgage Lending: Comparative Markets and Experience*
J. E. Morton PUP, 1956, 207 pp., $4.00

V Studies in Corporate Bond Financing

1 *The Volume of Corporate Bond Financing since 1900*
W. Braddock Hickman
PUP, 1953, 460 pp., $7.50

2 *Corporate Bond Quality and Investor Experience*
W. Braddock Hickman
PUP, 1958, 565 pp., $10.00

3 *Statistical Measures of Corporate Bond Financing since 1900*
W. Braddock Hickman
PUP, 1960, 612 pp., $9.00

VI Studies in Agricultural Financing

1 *Mortgage Lending Experience in Agriculture*
Lawrence A. Jones and David Durand
PUP, 1954, 255 pp., $5.00

2 *Patterns of Farm Financial Structure: A Cross-Section View of Economic and Physical Determinants*
Donald C. Horton PUP, 1957, 205 pp., $4.50

OTHER STUDIES

1 *The Pattern of Financial Asset Ownership: Wisconsin Individuals, 1949*
Thomas R. Atkinson PUP, 1956, 194 pp., $3.75

2 *Federal Lending and Loan Insurance*
Raymond J. Saulnier, Harold G. Halcrow, and Neil H. Jacoby PUP, 1958, 596 pp., $12.00

STUDIES IN INTERNATIONAL ECONOMIC RELATIONS

1 *Problems of the United States as World Trader and Banker*
Hal B. Lary PUP, 1963, 191 pp., $4.50

2 *Price and Quantity Trends in the Foreign Trade of the United States*
Robert E. Lipsey PUP, 1963, 505 pp., $10.00

STUDIES IN INCOME AND WEALTH

Conference on Research in Income and Wealth

*1 Eight papers on concepts and measurement of national income 1937, 366 pp.

*2 Six papers on wealth measurement, price changes, savings, capital gains, and government product UM, 1938, 354 pp.

*3 Seven papers on income size distribution, savings, national product, and distribution of income by states 1939, 502 pp.

*4 *Outlay and Income in the United States, 1921-1938*
Harold Barger 1942, 418 pp.

*5 *Income Size Distributions in the United States, Part I* 1943, 157 pp.

*6 Seven papers on income measurement, government product, parity, international transactions, forecasting national income, income differences among communities, and net capital formation 1943, 301 pp.

*7 *Changes in Income Distribution during the Great Depression*
Horst Mendershausen 1946, 191 pp.

*8 Eleven papers on estimating national income, for use in dealing with war problems and postwar adjustments 1946, 311 pp.

9 *Analysis of Wisconsin Income*
Frank A. Hanna, Joseph A. Pechman, Sidney M. Lerner CUP, 1948, 279 pp., $3.50

*10 Eight papers on standardizing basic concepts of national bookkeeping by American, British, and Canadian statisticians; problems of international comparisons of income and wealth; the nation's economic budget and forecasting gross national product and employment; savings and income distribution; and resource distribution patterns 1947, 351 pp.

*11 Six papers on the industrial distribution of manpower, real incomes in dissimilar geographic areas, national income forecasting, and the savings-income ratio 1949, 462 pp.

12 Thirteen papers on national wealth CUP, 1950, 599 pp., $6.00
Epstein's Paper

*13 Ten papers on size distribution of income 1951, 601 pp.

14 Seven papers on wealth, the value of reproducible tangible assets, the concentration of wealth, the Estates Survey, real property assets, and the relations of asset holdings to economic behavior and motivation CUP, 1951, 286 pp., $3.50

15 Eight papers on size distribution of income CUP, 1952, 240 pp., $3.50

16 *Long-Range Economic Projection* PUP, 1954, 486 pp., $9.00

*17 *Short-Term Economic Forecasting* UM, 1955, 517 pp.

18 *Input-Output Analysis: An Appraisal* PUP, 1955, 381 pp., $7.50

19 *Problems of Capital Formation: Concepts, Measurement, and Controlling Factors* PUP, 1957, 623 pp., $7.50

---

*Out of print.

20 *Problems in the International Comparison of Economic Accounts*
PUP, 1957, 414 pp., $8.00

21 *Regional Income*
PUP, 1957, 418 pp., $8.00

*22 *A Critique of the United States Income and Product Accounts*
1958, 599 pp.

23 *An Appraisal of the 1950 Census Income Data*
PUP, 1958, 460 pp., $10.00

24 *Trends in the American Economy in the Nineteenth Century*   PUP, 1960, 791 pp., $15.00

25 *Output, Input, and Productivity Measurement* (contains author and title indexes for Studies in Income and Wealth, Volumes 1-25)
PUP, 1961, 516 pp., $10.00

26 *The Flow-of-Funds Approach to Social Accounting*   PUP, UM, 1962, 497 pp., $10.00

27 *The Behavior of Income Shares: Selected Theoretical and Empirical Issues*
PUP, 1964, 404 pp., $8.00

28 *Models of Income Determination*
PUP, 1964, 436 pp., $10.00

29 *Measuring the Nation's Wealth*
CUP, 1964, 866 pp., $6.00

Conference on Price Research

*1 *Report of the Committee on Prices in the Bituminous Coal Industry*   1938, 164 pp.

*2 *Textile Markets: Their Structure in Relation to Price Research*   1939, 286 pp.

*3 *Price Research in the Steel and Petroleum Industries*   1939, 183 pp.

4 *Cost Behavior and Price Policy*
Committee on Price Determination
CUP, 1943, 375 pp., $3.00

5 *Minimum Price Fixing in the Bituminous Coal Industry*
Waldo E. Fisher and Charles M. James
PUP, 1955, 554 pp., $10.00

Special Conference Series

Universities—National Bureau Committee for Economic Research

*1 *Problems in the Study of Economic Growth*
UM, 1949

*2 *Conference on Business Cycles*
1951, 445 pp.

*Out of print.

3 *Conference on Research in Business Finance*
CUP, 1952, 358 pp., $5.00

4 *Regularization of Business Investment*
PUP, 1954, 539 pp., $8.00

5 *Business Concentration and Price Policy*
PUP, 1955, 524 pp., $9.00

6 *Capital Formation and Economic Growth*
PUP, 1955, 690 pp., $12.00

*7 *Policies to Combat Depression*
UM, 1956, 427 pp.

8 *The Measurement and Behavior of Unemployment*
PUP, 1957, 615 pp., $7.50

9 *Problems in International Economics*
CUP, 1958, 142 pp., $1.50
February 1958 Supplement to the *Review of Economics and Statistics.*

10 *The Quality and Economic Significance of Anticipations Data*
PUP, 1960, 477 pp., $9.00

11 *Demographic and Economic Change in Developed Countries*
PUP, 1960, 547 pp., $12.00

12 *Public Finances: Needs, Sources, and Utilization*
PUP, 1961, 526 pp., $10.00

13 *The Rate and Direction of Inventive Activity: Economic and Social Factors*
PUP, 1962, 646 pp., $12.50

14 *Aspects of Labor Economics*
PUP, 1962, 361 pp., $7.50

15 *Investment in Human Beings*
CUP, 1962, 157 pp., $1.95
October 1962 Supplement to the *Journal of Political Economy.*

16 *The State of Monetary Economics*
CUP, 1963, 155 pp., $2.00
February 1963 Supplement to the *Review of Economics and Statistics.*

Other Conferences

1 *Consumer Instalment Credit: Conference on Regulation*
Order from Superintendent of Documents, Washington, D.C. 10025
1957, Vol. 1, 569 pp., $1.75
1957, Vol. 2, 171 pp., 60¢

2 *Philanthropy and Public Policy*
CUP, 1962, 155 pp., $2.50

3 *The Role of Direct and Indirect Taxes in the Federal Revenue System*
A Conference Report of the National Bureau of Economic Research and the Brookings Institution
PUP, 1964, 333 pp., $7.50
(paperbound, $2.95, order from PUP only)

EXPLORATORY REPORTS

1 *Research in Securities Markets*
Exploratory Committee on Research in Securities Markets   CUP, 1946, 34 pp., 50¢

2 *Research in the Capital and Securities Markets*
Exploratory Committee on Research in the Capital and Securities Markets
CUP, 1954, 88 pp., $1.00

3 *Suggestions for Research in the Economics of Pensions*
CUP, 1957, 64 pp., $1.00

4 *The Comparative Study of Economic Growth and Structure: Suggestions on Research Objectives and Organization*
CUP, 1959, 201 pp., $3.00

5 *Research in the Capital Markets* May 1964
Supplement to the *Journal of Finance*
CUP, 1964, 48 pp., $1.00

BULLETINS

(Replaced by Occasional Papers, December 1949. Those listed are available; a complete list is included in the 25th Annual Report.)

42 *Aspects of the Price Recession of 1929-1931*
Frederick C. Mills   CUP, 1931, 25¢

47 *Employment during the Depression*
Meredith B. Givens   CUP, 1933, 25¢

48 *Aspects of Recent Price Movements*
Frederick C. Mills   CUP, 1933, 25¢

49 *National Income, 1929-1932*
Simon Kuznets   CUP, 1934, 25¢

51 *Recent Changes in Production*
Charles A. Bliss   CUP, 1934, 25¢

52 *Gross Capital Formation, 1919-1933*
Simon Kuznets   CUP, 1934, 50¢

53 *Changes in Prices, Manufacturing Costs and Industrial Productivity, 1929-1934*
Frederick C. Mills   CUP, 1934, 25¢

54 *Wages and Hours under the Codes of Fair Competition*
Leo Wolman   CUP, 1935, 25¢

56 *Aspects of Manufacturing Operations during Recovery*
Frederick C. Mills   CUP, 1935, 50¢

57 *The National Bureau's Measures of Cyclical Behavior*
Wesley C. Mitchell and Arthur F. Burns
CUP, 1935, 50¢

59 *Income Originating in Nine Basic Industries, 1913-1934*
Simon Kuznets   CUP, 1936, 50¢

60 *Measures of Capital Consumption, 1919-1933*
Solomon Fabricant   CUP, 1936, 25¢

69 *Statistical Indicators of Cyclical Revivals*
Wesley C. Mitchell and Arthur F. Burns
CUP, 1938, 25¢

70 *Employment Opportunities in Manufacturing Industries of the United States*
Frederick C. Mills   CUP, 1938, 25¢

76-77 *The Statistical Pattern of Instalment Debt*
R. A. Young and Blanche Bernstein
CUP, 1939, 50¢

79 *The Volume of Consumer Instalment Credit, 1929-1938*
Duncan McC. Holthausen, Malcolm L. Merriam, and Rolf Nugent   CUP, 1940, 25¢

OCCASIONAL PAPERS

*1 *Manufacturing Output, 1929-1937*
Solomon Fabricant   1940, 28 pp.

*2 *National Income, 1919-1938*
Simon Kuznets   1941, 32 pp.

*3 *Finished Commodities since 1879: Output and Its Composition*
William H. Shaw   1941, 49 pp.

*4 *The Relation between Factory Employment and Output since 1899*
Solomon Fabricant   1941, 39 pp.

*5 *Railway Freight Traffic in Prosperity and Depression*
Thor Hultgren   1942, 51 pp.

*6 *Uses of National Income in Peace and War*
Simon Kuznets   1942, 42 pp.

*7 *Productivity of Labor in Peace and War*
Solomon Fabricant   UM, 1942, 28 pp.

*8 *The Banking System and War Finance*
Charles R. Whittlesey   1943, 53 pp.

*9 *Wartime 'Prosperity' and the Future*
Wesley C. Mitchell   1943, 40 pp.

10 *The Effect of War on Business Financing: Manufacturing and Trade, World War I*
Charles H. Schmidt and Ralph A. Young
CUP, 1943, 95 pp., 50¢

11 *The Effect of War on Currency and Deposits*
Charles R. Whittlesey   CUP, 1943, 50 pp., 35¢

*12 *Prices in a War Economy: Some Aspects of the Present Price Structure of the United States*
Frederick C. Mills   1943, 102 pp.

*13 *Railroad Travel and the State of Business*
Thor Hultgren   1943, 35 pp.

---

*Out of print.

14 *The Labor Force in Wartime America*
Clarence D. Long   CUP, 1944, 73 pp., 50¢

15 *Railway Traffic Expansion and Use of Resources in World War II*
Thor Hultgren   CUP, 1944, 31 pp., 35¢

*16 *British and American Plans for International Currency Stabilization*
J. H. Riddle   1943, 42 pp.

*17 *Natural Product, War and Prewar*
Simon Kuznets   1944, 54 pp.

18 *Production of Industrial Materials in World Wars I and II*
Geoffrey H. Moore   CUP, 1944, 81 pp., 50¢

19 *Canada's Financial System in War*
Benjamin H. Higgins   CUP, 1944, 82 pp., 50¢

*20 *Nazi War Finance and Banking*
Otto Nathan   UM, 1944, 100 pp.

*21 *The Federal Reserve System in Wartime*
Anna Youngman   1945, 67 pp.

*22 *Bank Liquidity and the War*
Charles R. Whittlesey   1945, 86 pp.

*23 *Labor Savings in American Industry, 1899-1939*
Solomon Fabricant   1945, 56 pp.

24 *Domestic Servants in the United States, 1900-1940*
George J. Stigler   CUP, 1946, 44 pp., 50¢

*25 *Recent Developments in Dominion-Provincial Fiscal Relations in Canada*
J. A. Maxwell   UM, 1948, 62 pp.

*26 *The Role of Inventories in Business Cycles*
Moses Abramovitz   1948, 26 pp.

27 *The Structure of Postwar Prices*
Frederick C. Mills   CUP, 1948, 66 pp., 75¢

28 *Lombard Street in War and Reconstruction*
Benjamin H. Higgins CUP, 1949, 115 pp., $1.00

*29 *The Rising Trend of Government Employment*
Solomon Fabricant   1949, 30 pp.

30 *Costs and Returns on Farm Mortgage Lending by Life Insurance Companies, 1945-1947*
R. J. Saulnier   CUP, 1949, 55 pp., $1.00

*31 *Statistical Indicators of Cyclical Revivals and Recessions*
Geoffrey H. Moore   1950, 96 pp.

*32 *Cyclical Diversities in the Fortunes of Industrial Corporations*
Thor Hultgren   1950, 34 pp.

33 *Employment and Compensation in Education*
George J. Stigler   CUP, 1950, 77 pp., $1.00

*34 *Behavior of Wage Rates during Business Cycles*
Daniel Creamer   1950, 66 pp.

35 *Shares of Upper Income Groups in Income and Savings*
Simon Kuznets   CUP, 1950, 68 pp., $1.00

36 *The Labor Force in War and Transition: Four Countries*
Clarence D. Long   CUP, 1952, 61 pp., $1.00

*37 *Trends and Cycles in Corporate Bond Financing*
W. Braddock Hickman   1952, 37 pp.

*38 *Productivity and Economic Progress*
Frederick C. Mills   1952, 36 pp.

*39 *The Role of Federal Credit Aids in Residential Construction*
Leo Grebler   1953, 76 pp.

*40 *Transport and the State of Trade in Britain*
Thor Hultgren   1953, 126 pp.

*41 *Capital and Output Trends in Manufacturing Industries, 1880-1948*
Daniel Creamer   1954, 104 pp.

*42 *The Share of Financial Intermediaries in National Wealth and National Assets, 1900-1949*
Raymond W. Goldsmith   1954, 120 pp.

*43 *Trends and Cycles in Capital Formation by United States Railroads, 1870-1950*
Melville J. Ulmer   1954, 70 pp.

*44 *The Growth of Physical Capital in Agriculture, 1870-1950*
Alvin S. Tostlebe   1954, 104 pp.

45 *Capital and Output Trends in Mining Industries, 1870-1948*
Israel Borenstein   CUP, 1954, 81 pp., $1.00

46 *Immigration and the Foreign Born*
Simon Kuznets and Ernest Rubin
CUP, 1954, 119 pp., $1.50

*47 *The Ownership of Tax-Exempt Securities, 1913-1953*
George E. Lent   1955, 150 pp.

*48 *A Century and a Half of Federal Expenditures*
M. Slade Kendrick   1955, 112 pp.

49 *The Korean War and United States Economic Activity, 1950-1952*
Bert G. Hickman   CUP, 1955, 72 pp., 75¢

50 *Agricultural Equipment Financing*
Howard G. Diesslin CUP, 1955, 116 pp., $1.25

51 *Interest as a Source of Personal Income and Tax Revenue*
Lawrence H. Seltzer CUP, 1955, 82 pp., $1.25

*52 *Resource and Output Trends in the United States since 1870*
Moses Abramovitz   1956, 23 pp.

*53 *Productivity Trends: Capital and Labor*
John W. Kendrick   1956, 23 pp.

*54 *Bank Stock Prices and the Bank Capital Problem*
David Durand   1957, 86 pp.

55 *Some Observations on Soviet Industrial Growth*
G. Warren Nutter   CUP, 1957, 12 pp., 50¢

56 *Distribution of Union Membership among the States, 1939 and 1953*
Leo Troy   CUP, 1957, 40 pp., 75¢

―――
*Out of Print.

57 *Electronic Computers and Business Indicators*
Julius Shiskin   CUP, 1957, 52 pp., $1.00

*58 *Federal Lending: Its Growth and Impact*
A summary, prepared by the National Bureau's editorial staff, of *Federal Lending and Loan Insurance,* by R. J. Saulnier, Harold G. Halcrow, Neil H. Jacoby   1957, 56 pp.

59 *Corporate Bonds: Quality and Investment Performance*
W. Braddock Hickman   CUP, 1957, 43 pp., 75¢

*60 *The Postwar Rise of Mortgage Companies*
Saul B. Klaman   1959, 117 pp.

*61 *Measuring Recessions*
Geoffrey H. Moore   1958, 57 pp.

*62 *The Demand for Currency Relative to Total Money Supply*
Phillip Cagan   1958, 37 pp.

63 *Basic Facts on Productivity Change*
Solomon Fabricant   CUP, 1959, 57 pp., $1.00

64 *The Role of Middleman Transactions in World Trade*
Robert M. Lichtenberg
                      CUP, 1959, 102 pp., $1.50

65 *Freight Transportation in the Soviet Union: A Comparison with the United States*
Ernest W. Williams, Jr. CUP, 1959, 47 pp., 75¢

*66 *City Expenditures in the United States*
Harvey E. Brazer   UM, 1959, 93 pp.

67 *Trade Balances during Business Cycles: U.S. and Britain since 1880*
Ilse Mintz   CUP, 1959, 109 pp., $1.50

68 *The Demand for Money: Some Theoretical and Empirical Results*
Milton Friedman   CUP, 1959, 25 pp., 75¢

*69 *The Average Workweek as an Economic Indicator*
Gerhard Bry   1959, 122 pp.

*70 *Consumer Expectations, Plans, and Purchases: a Progress Report*
F. Thomas Juster   1959, 192 pp.

*71 *Changes in the Share of Wealth Held by Top Wealth-Holders, 1922-1956*
Robert J. Lampman   1960, 32 pp.

72 *Housing Issues in Economic Stabilization Policy*
Leo Grebler   CUP, 1960, 140 pp., $1.50

73 *Regional Cycles of Manufacturing Employment in the United States, 1914-1953*
George H. Borts   CUP, 1960, 60 pp., 75¢

*74 *Changes in Labor Cost During Cycles in Production and Business*
Thor Hultgren   1960, 102 pp.

75 *New Measures of Wage-Earner Compensation in Manufacturing, 1914-57*
Albert Rees   CUP, 1960, 35 pp., 75¢

76 *American Exports During Business Cycles, 1879-1958*
Ilse Mintz   CUP, 1961, 104 pp., $1.00

77 *Signals of Recession and Recovery: An Experiment with Monthly Reporting*
Julius Shiskin   CUP, 1961, 203 pp., $3.00

78 *The Postwar Rise in the Velocity of Money: A Sectoral Analysis*
Richard T. Selden   CUP, 1962, 72 pp., $1.00

*†79 *The American Baby Boom in Historical Perspective*
Richard A. Easterlin   1962, 64 pp.

80 *Small-Scale Industry in the Soviet Union*
Adam Kaufman   CUP, 1962, 111 pp., $2.00

81 *The United States Savings Bond Program in the Postwar Period*
George Hanc   CUP, 1962, 122 pp., $1.50

82 *The Quality of Bank Loans: A Study of Bank Examination Records*
Albert M. Wojnilower CUP, 1962, 88 pp., $1.50

83 *Cost of Providing Consumer Credit: A Study of Four Major Types of Financial Institutions*
Paul Smith   CUP, 1962, 32 pp., 50¢

84 *Unfilled Orders, Price Changes, and Business Fluctuations*
Victor Zarnowitz   CUP, 1962, 32 pp., 75¢

85 *Trends and Cycles in the Commercial Paper Market*
Richard T. Selden   CUP, 1963, 133 pp., $1.75

86 *New-Automobile Finance Rates, 1924-62*
Robert P. Shay   CUP, 1963, 37 pp., 75¢

87 *The Quality of Trade Credit*
Martin H. Seiden   CUP, 1964, 149 pp., $3.00

88 *Consumer Sensitivity to Finance Rates: An Empirical and Analytical Investigation*
F. Thomas Juster and Robert P. Shay
                    CUP, 1964, 116 pp., $2.50

89 *Productivity Trends in the Goods and Services Sectors, 1929-61: A Preliminary Survey*
Victor R. Fuchs   CUP, 1964, 57 pp., $1.75

90 *Evidences of Long Swings in Aggregate Construction Since the Civil War*
Moses Abramovitz CUP, 1964, 252 pp., $4.00

91 *The Cyclical Behavior of the Term Structure of Interest Rates*
Reuben A. Kessel   CUP, 1965, 125 pp., $3.00

92 *Trade Union Membership, 1897-1962*
Leo Troy   CUP, 1965, 90 pp., $2.00

93 *Financial Adjustments to Unemployment*
Philip A. Klein   CUP, 1965, 88 pp., $2.50

TECHNICAL PAPERS

*1 *A Significance Test for Time Series and Other Ordered Observations*
W. Allen Wallis and Geoffrey H. Moore
                                1941, 59 pp.

---

*Out of print.
†Reprinted in the Bobbs-Merrill Reprint Series in the Social Sciences, S-381.

*2 *The Relation of Cost to Output for a Leather Belt Shop*
Joel Dean   1941, 72 pp.

*3 *Basic Yields of Corporate Bonds, 1900-1942*
David Durand   1942, 34 pp.

*4 *Currency Held by the Public, the Banks, and the Treasury, Monthly, December 1917-December 1944*
Anna Jacobson Schwartz and Elma Oliver
                                            1947, 65 pp.

*5 *Concerning a New Federal Financial Statement*
Morris A. Copeland   1947, 63 pp.

*6 *Basic Yields of Bonds, 1926-1947: Their Measurement and Pattern*
David Durand and Willis J. Winn
                                       UM, 1947, 40 pp.

7 *Factors Affecting the Demand for Consumer Instalment Sales Credit*
Avram Kisselgoff   CUP, 1952, 70 pp., $1.50

*8 *A Study of Aggregate Consumption Functions*
Robert Ferber   1953, 72 pp.

9 *The Volume of Residential Construction, 1889-1950*
David M. Blank   CUP, 1954, 111 pp., $1.50

*10 *Factors Influencing Consumption: An Experimental Analysis of Shoe Buying*
Ruth P. Mack   1954, 124 pp.

11 *Fiscal-Year Reporting for Corporate Income Tax*
W. L. Crum   CUP, 1956, 65 pp., $1.25

12 *Seasonal Adjustments by Electronic Computer Methods*
Julius Shiskin and Harry Eisenpress
                        CUP, 1958, 34 pp., 75¢

*13 *The Volume of Mortgage Debt in the Postwar Decade*
Saul B. Klaman   1958, 158 pp.

14 *Industrial Demands upon the Money Market, 1919-57: A Study in Fund-Flow Analysis*
Wilson F. Payne   CUP, 1961, 158 pp., $1.50

15 *Methods for Improving World Transportation Accounts, Applied to 1950-1953*
Herman F. Karreman
                        CUP, 1961, 138 pp., $1.50

16 *The Interpolation of Times Series by Related Series*
Milton Friedman   CUP, 1962, 33 pp., 75¢

17 *Estimates of Residential Building, United States, 1840-1939*
Manuel Gottlieb   CUP, 1964, 115 pp., $2.00

18 *The Measurement of Corporate Sources and Uses of Funds*
David Meiselman and Eli Shapiro
                        CUP, 1964, 297 pp., $4.50

ANNUAL REPORTS (gratis)

(Order from NBER)

25th *The National Bureau's First Quarter-Century*
                                            May 1945

*26th *Economic Research and the Keynesian Thinking of Our Times*   June 1946

*27th *Stepping Stones Towards the Future*
                                        UM, March 1947

28th *The Cumulation of Economic Knowledge*
                                            May 1948

29th *Wesley Mitchell and the National Bureau*
                                            May 1949

*30th *New Facts on Business Cycles*
                                        UM, May 1950

31st *Looking Forward*   May 1951

32nd *The Instability of Consumer Spending*
                                            May 1952

*33rd *Business Cycle Research and the Needs of Our Times*   UM, May 1953

*34th *Economic Progress and Economic Change*
                                        UM, May 1954

35th *Government in Economic Life*   May 1955

*36th *Basic Research and the Analysis of Current Business Conditions*   May 1956

37th *Financial Research and the Problems of the Day*   May 1957

38th *Investing in Economic Knowledge*   May 1958

39th *The Study of Economic Growth*   May 1959

40th *A Respect for Facts*   May 1960

*41st *Towards a Firmer Basis of Economic Policy*
                                            May 1961

42nd *Tested Knowledge of Business Cycles*
                                           June 1962

43rd *The Uses of Economic Research*   May 1963

44th *The National Bureau Enters Its Forty-Fifth Year*   June 1964

45th *The Task of Economics*   June 1965

---

*Out of print.

115

CONTRIBUTIONS AND SUBSCRIPTIONS

Contributors or subscribers of $75 or more a year are entitled to receive a complimentary copy of each publication — books, Occasional Papers, Technical Papers, and the Annual Report — in advance of release to the public. In addition, the subscriber is entitled to a 33-1/3 per cent discount on any National Bureau publication purchased.

A special subscription rate of $35, providing the same privileges as above, is open to faculty members and students of recognized educational institutions. A limited faculty-student rate of $5, open to faculty members and students of recognized educational institutions, entitles the subscriber to a complimentary copy of each Occasional Paper, Technical Paper, and the Annual Report and to a 40 per cent discount on any publication purchased.

For those who wish to subscribe only to Occasional Papers and Technical Papers, the subscription rate is $4 for five issues. A subscriber of $4 receives the next five *papers* and the annual report.

Send contributions or subscriptions, or address inquiries, to the National Bureau's Executive Director, William J. Carson.

*Contributions to the National Bureau are
deductible in calculating income taxes.*

HOW NATIONAL BUREAU PUBLICATIONS ARE DISTRIBUTED

Effective September 1, 1964 Columbia University Press became the distributor to nonsubscribers of the National Bureau's books published prior to 1953 and since September 1, 1964, and of its Occasional Papers and Technical Papers.

Princeton University Press is the distributor to nonsubscribers of the National Bureau's books published by it between 1953 and September 1, 1964.

The National Bureau itself is the distributor to subscribers of books and papers.

HOW TO ORDER PUBLICATIONS

Orders for publications of the National Bureau should be transmitted as follows (if mail address is New York City, include 4 per cent sales tax with all remittances on all orders to National Bureau and to Columbia University Press):

SUBSCRIBERS: Order from National Bureau, 261 Madison Avenue, New York, N. Y. 10016, all books and papers.

NONSUBSCRIBERS: Order from Columbia University Press, 2960 Broadway, New York, N. Y. 10027: (1) Occasional Papers and Technical Papers, and (2) books published prior to 1953 and subsequent to September 1, 1964.

Order from Princeton University Press, Princeton, New Jersey, books published between 1953 and September 1, 1964.

The preceding section, "National Bureau Publications," shows the distributor of each publication.